Best Easy Day Hikes
Pittsburgh

Help Us Keep This Guide Up to Date

Every effort has been made by the author and editors to make this guide as accurate and useful as possible. However, many things can change after a guide is published—trails are rerouted, regulations change, facilities come under new management, etc.

We would love to hear from you concerning your experiences with this guide and how you feel it could be improved and kept up to date. While we may not be able to respond to all comments and suggestions, we'll take them to heart and we'll also make certain to share them with the author. Please send your comments and suggestions to the following address:

The Globe Pequot Press
Reader Response/Editorial Department
P.O. Box 480
Guilford, CT 06437

Or you may e-mail us at:

editorial@GlobePequot.com

Thanks for your input, and happy trails!

Best Easy Day Hikes Series

Best Easy Day Hikes
Pittsburgh

Bob Frye

FALCONGUIDES

GUILFORD, CONNECTICUT
HELENA, MONTANA

AN IMPRINT OF GLOBE PEQUOT PRESS

FALCONGUIDES®

Copyright © 2009 by Morris Book Publishing, LLC

Falcon, FalconGuides, and Outfit Your Mind are registered trademarks
of Morris Book Publishing, LLC.

TOPO! Explorer software and SuperQuad source maps courtesy of National
Geographic Maps. For information about TOPO! Explorer, TOPO!, and Nat Geo
Maps products, go to www.topo.com or www.natgeomaps.com.

Maps © Morris Book Publishing, LLC

Library of Congress Cataloging-in-Publication Data
Frye, Bob, 1967-
  Best easy day hikes, Pittsburgh / Bob Frye.
     p. cm. — (Falconguides)
  ISBN 978-0-7627-5438-0
  1. Hiking–Pennsylvania—Pittsburgh Region–Guidebooks. 2. Pitts-
burgh Region (Pa.)—Guidebooks. I. Title.
  GV199.42.P42P67 2009
  917.48'86–dc22
                                                    2009023975
Printed in the United States of America

10 9 8 7 6 5 4 3 2 1

Contents

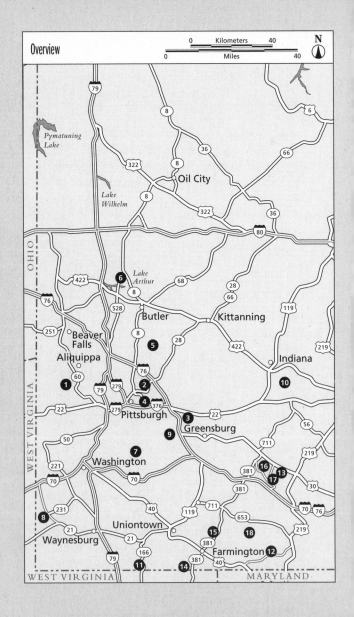

Overview

0 Kilometers 40

0 Miles 40

N

Pymatuning Lake

Oil City

Lake Wilhelm

OHIO

Lake Arthur

Butler

Kittanning

Beaver Falls

Aliquippa

Indiana

WEST VIRGINIA

Pittsburgh

Greensburg

Washington

Uniontown

Waynesburg

Farmington

WEST VIRGINIA

MARYLAND

Acknowledgments

Western Pennsylvania in general, and the Pittsburgh region in particular, is blessed with amazing beauty. Exciting wildlife, dazzling waterfalls, wildflowers that boast glorious colors, and amazing vistas make each trip into the outdoors a wonderful experience.

A large and well-maintained network of trails makes it easy to take in all of the best that nature has to offer, too. Thanks for that goes to a lot of people.

Trail volunteers give up weekends to saw through blowdowns, build bridges, and map out routes for the rest of us. State park and forest crews, county and city park staff, Historical and Museum Commission employees, and those in the employ of federal agencies like the National Park Service map out, build, and maintain trails, even though they're often burdened with budgets too small to cover needs. The Pennsylvania Game Commission, meanwhile, is funded solely by the sale of hunting licenses—it gets no general tax revenue—but allows hikers, bikers, birders, and others who never pick up a firearm to use its game lands free of charge, too.

To all those people, we who love to hike say thank you.

Introduction

To walk the woods and fields that surround Pittsburgh today is to walk a country that has been alternately beautiful and besmirched.

When the first European settlers arrived on the shores of America, more than 90 percent of Pennsylvania's nearly twenty-nine million acres were forested. Those woods were impressive, too. Towering virgin trees 100 to 150 feet tall covered the landscape, giant sentinels overlooking natural cathedrals in every valley and on every ridgetop.

Things stayed that way for a long while, too. With the Allegheny Mountains a formidable obstacle, large predators like bears and mountain lions roaming the land, and Native Americans clinging to what they saw as their own territory, homesteaders were slow to migrate west. As late as the days of America's war for independence, Pittsburgh was on the edge of the nation's wild, woolly, and still largely untouched frontier.

A century later that was anything but the case.

By the end of the Civil War, America was fast becoming an industrialized nation, and Pittsburgh was at the dirty, calloused, blackened heart of that. It was producing half of the glass and 40 percent of the iron consumed by the country annually. That alone required burning three million tons of coal each year.

The impact on the region's environment was truly devastating.

With no environmental laws in place—indeed, the courts frowned on any ruling that threatened the economic tides—heavy industry devoured the surrounding countryside without pause. Night and day, rivers were defiled, mountains were debased, and the people who lived here were left to suffer the consequences.

"Pittsburgh," wrote nineteenth-century author Willard Glazier, "is a smoky, dismal city at her best. At her worst, nothing darker, dingier or more dispiriting can be imagined . . . the smoke from her dwellings, stores, factories, foundries and steamboats, uniting, settles in a cloud over the narrow valley in which she is built, until the very sun looks coppery through the sooty haze."

Boston writer James Parton was even more succinct in describing Pittsburgh after a visit in 1868. He called the city "hell with the lid off."

Fortunately for those who enjoy the outdoors, things have changed dramatically.

Pittsburgh may not be the edge of the frontier anymore, but no longer is it the city whose rivers were once so polluted that they occasionally caught fire either. The death, or at least radical amputation, of the city's steel industry beginning in the 1970s was a decade-long, agonizing bloodletting. Families built on paychecks from the mills suffered enormously.

But the result has been a startlingly clean city and region. They sparkle now like a white diamond forged from black coal under enormous pressure.

Today, you can roam second-generation forests that cover tens of thousands of acres. Wildlife—white-tailed deer, black bears, coyotes, squirrels, otters, and fishers, to name a few species—are again abundant. Many of the streams that were once devoid of life support everything from crayfish to brook trout. There's even wilderness to be had. Follow the dirt roads to Quebec Run, south of the city, and you'll find beauty as rugged and wild as anywhere.

History? Solitude? Nature programming? The area has hikes that offer them all, too.

That's perhaps the greatest thing about this region. It's cliché to suggest that any region has "a little bit of something for everyone," but if that holds true for hikers anywhere, this is that place.

I know that. Born and raised in western Pennsylvania, I've spent a lifetime roaming its fields and forests, and the beauty of this place still stuns me at times. Some of the hikes in this book are old favorites of mine. Others are new. Without exception, I found something at each that made me stop and say, "Oh, wow."

Hopefully, you'll be equally impressed with what you see out there.

Your opportunities to find something you might like are certainly many. Pennsylvania offers three- and, in some cases, four-season hiking. There are exceptions, of course, but you can generally count on mild spring temperatures arriving by April and Indian summer lasting until October or even November.

Winter is a little iffier. The mountains of the Laurel Highlands and the regions north of Pittsburgh get more rain, snow, and fog, and they get it earlier than the city itself does. The roads leading to trailheads in those places can sometimes be treacherous or even impassable, too. But many of these hikes can be done year-round. And if you're willing to walk in snowshoes, almost anything's possible.

There's plenty to see, too. Much of western Pennsylvania is covered by what is known as Appalachian oak forest. It's dominated by white, red, and chestnut oaks, hickories, and white pines. Farther north, however, northern hardwood forests of hemlocks, black cherry, and American beech are more common. The western edge of the state offers more sugar maples, black walnuts, and basswood, while the southernmost tip gives you the chance to walk under the leaves of species that are relatively rare north of the Mason-Dixon Line, like yellow buckeye.

State parks offer a good network of trails, though some are of the shorter variety. If you want a longer walk, you often have to combine a few trails. That's not always bad, though. If you want to combine a hike with a picnic at a place that offers tables, primitive restrooms, and charcoal grills, these are good bets.

State forests are home to some of the state's longer hiking trails. Don't come expecting to be pampered. Amenities here are comparatively few. But if all you need is a place to park, a blazed trail, and some solitude, there is some real beauty to be had.

With a few exceptions, state game lands don't have much in the way of "official" hiking trails. That's because they were bought and are maintained with money generated by the sale of hunting licenses. The Pennsylvania Game Commission gets no general tax money, so if you don't hunt, you don't add acres to the game lands system or take care of what already exists. Understandably then, these lands are managed primarily for hunters and wildlife. Hikers can and do make heavy use of them, however, in between hunting seasons.

City and county parks are like state parks in the sense that they try to serve the greatest variety of people. That means trails often get neither more nor less attention than playgrounds, soccer fields, and horseshoe pits. Some excellent trails do exist, however.

Is all of that enough to convince you to get outside and try walking your way around western Pennsylvania? I certainly hope so. This is a wonderful place to live, work—and especially play.

But you'll see that for yourself once you lace up your boots and get out there, so pick a trail and take off. You'll be glad you did.

Weather

The Pittsburgh area is blessed with a variable, four-season climate, with rainy and dry seasons, warm and cold ones. Just about the time you're sick of snow, spring breaks. When you can't take the heat anymore, fall arrives. And so on.

While overall that weather is inviting, each season poses unique challenges for hikers.

Spring, namely April and May, brings the most rain. June through September are drier and warmer, while October and November are the cooler months of fall. December through March are the coldest months, when snow is frequent and temperatures can drop to zero and lower.

Those are just general guidelines, though. It pays to remember that the conditions in Pittsburgh will not necessarily be the same as the conditions on top of the Laurel Mountains or in the foothills to the southwest at the same time on the same day. The Laurel Mountains in particular get considerably more rain, fog, and snow—especially snow. When the streets in Pittsburgh are clear and dry, the roads leading to trailheads in the mountains can be snow-packed and essentially closed for all but those with the stoutest of four-wheel-drive vehicles. The trails themselves will be equally rough, perhaps to the point of requiring snowshoes.

The key to comfortable hiking most of the time is to dress in layers. Carry a pack so that if things are colder than expected, you can pull out a hat and gloves and an extra sweater to bundle up. If things are warmer than you thought they'd be, you can shed a layer or two.

The greatest danger a hiker faces on hot summer days is dehydration. No matter the trail's length or the amount of shade along the route, carry plenty of water. When the temperatures soar, avoid hiking in the heat of the day. Morning and evening hours offer lovely light and a greater opportunity to see wildlife, while mitigating the risks of heat-related illness.

Critters

You'll encounter mostly benign, sweet creatures on these trails, such as white-tailed deer; gray, fox, and red squirrels; chipmunks; rabbits; wild turkeys; and a variety of songbirds. More rarely seen (during the daylight hours especially) are bobcats, raccoons, and opossums. Deer in some of the parks are remarkably tame and may linger on or close to the trail as you approach.

The countryside around Pittsburgh, particularly when you get into the Laurel Highlands, is also habitat for black bears, coyotes, and timber rattlesnakes. Massasauga rattlesnakes can be found at Jennings Environmental Education Center, too. Encounters are infrequent, but you should be prepared to react properly if you run across any of the above. Snakes generally only strike if they are threatened. You are too big to be dinner, so they typically avoid contact with humans. Keep your distance and they will keep theirs. If you come across a bear, make yourself as big as possible. Don't run or position yourself between a mother bear and her cubs. Bears are generally not aggressive and will flee if given the chance. If you don't act like or look like prey, they'll leave you alone. Coyotes are shy, and you'll be lucky to see one.

Be Prepared

Hiking in Pittsburgh and its surrounding countryside is generally safe. Still, hikers should be prepared, whether they are going out for a short stroll through Todd Nature Reserve or venturing into the secluded Quebec Run Wild Area for a day-long expedition. Some specific advice:

- Know the basics of first aid, including how to treat bleeding, bites and stings, and fractures, strains, or sprains. Pack a first-aid kit on each excursion.

- Familiarize yourself with the symptoms of heat exhaustion and heat stroke. Heat exhaustion symptoms include heavy sweating, muscle cramps, headache, dizziness, and fainting. Should you or any of your hiking party exhibit any of these symptoms, cool the victim down immediately by rehydrating and getting him or her to an air-conditioned location. Cold showers also help reduce body temperature. Heat stroke is much more serious: The victim may lose consciousness and the skin is hot and dry to the touch. In this event, call 911 immediately.

- Regardless of the weather, your body needs a lot of water while hiking. A full 32-ounce bottle is the minimum for these short hikes, but more is always better. Bring a full water bottle, whether water is available along the trail or not.

- Don't drink from streams, rivers, creeks, or lakes without treating or filtering the water first. Waterways and water bodies may host a variety of contaminants, including giardia, which can cause serious intestinal unrest.

- Prepare for extremes of both heat and cold by dressing in layers.

- Carry a backpack in which you can store extra clothing, ample drinking water and food, and whatever goodies, like guidebooks, cameras, and binoculars, you might want.

- Some area trails have cell phone coverage. Bring your device, but make sure you've turned it off or have it on the vibrate setting while hiking. There's nothing like a "wake the dead" loud ring to startle every creature, including fellow hikers.

- Keep children under careful watch. Rivers and even rain-swollen creeks can have dangerous currents. Hazards along some of the trails include poison oak, uneven footing, and steep drop-offs; make sure children don't stray from the designated route. Children should carry a plastic whistle; if they become lost, they should stay in one place and blow the whistle to summon help.

Zero Impact

Trails in the Pittsburgh area, the Laurel Highlands, and other areas nearby are heavily used year-round. We, as trail users and advocates, must be especially vigilant to make sure our passage leaves no lasting mark. Here are some basic guidelines for preserving trails in the region:

- Pack out all your own trash, including biodegradable items like orange peels. You might also pack out garbage left by less considerate hikers.

- Don't approach or feed any wild creatures—the gray squirrel eyeing your snack food is best able to survive if it remains self-reliant.

- Don't pick wildflowers or gather rocks, antlers, feathers, and other treasures along the trail. Removing these items will only take away from the next hiker's experience.

- Avoid damaging trailside soils and plants by remaining on the established route. This is also a good rule of thumb for avoiding poison oak and stinging nettle, common regional trailside irritants.

- Don't cut switchbacks, which can promote erosion.

- Be courteous by not making loud noises while hiking.

- Many of these trails are multiuse, which means you'll share them with other hikers, trail runners, mountain bikers, and equestrians. Familiarize yourself with the proper trail etiquette, yielding the trail when appropriate.

- Use outhouses at trailheads or along the trail.

Pittsburgh Area Boundaries and Corridors

For the purposes of this guide, best easy day hikes are confined to a two-hour drive from downtown Pittsburgh. The hikes stretch from those within the city limits, like in Frick Park, to some in the mountains of the Laurel Highlands, the foothills of Greene County, and the countryside in between.

A number of major highways and interstates converge in Pittsburgh. Directions to trailheads are given from these arteries. They include Interstate 79 (north–south), Interstate 76 (east–west), U.S. Highways 30 and 22 (east–west), U.S. Highway 119 (north–south), and U.S. Highway 40 (east–west).

Land Management

The following government and private organizations manage most of the public lands described in this guide, and can provide further information on these hikes and other trails in their service areas.

Pennsylvania Department of Conservation and Natural Resources (Bureau of State Parks and Bureau of Forestry), Rachel Carson State Office Building, P.O. Box 8767, 400 Market Street, Harrisburg 17105-8767; (888) 727-2757; www.dcnr.state.pa.us; ra-askdcnr.state.pa.us. A complete listing of state parks and state forests is available on the Web site, along with park brochures and maps.

Pittsburgh Parks Conservancy, 2000 Technology Drive, Suite 300, Pittsburgh 15219; (412) 682-7275; www.pitts burghparks.org. A complete list of city parks is available online, along with maps, a calendar of events, and more.

Audubon Society of Western Pennsylvania, 614 Dorseyville Road, Pittsburgh 15238; (412) 963-6100; www .aswp.org. Directions and trail guides for both Beechwood Farms Nature Reserve and Todd Nature Reserve can be found on the group's Web site, along with an events calendar, live weather reports, and more.

Pennsylvania Game Commission, Southwest Region Office, 4820 Route 711, Bolivar 15923; (724) 238-9523;

www.pgc.state.pa.us. Maps of most state game lands, like Game Lands 302 at Enlow Fork, are available online. There's also lots of information about the wildlife you can expect to see in "Penn's Woods."

Regional trails in the area include the 70-mile Laurel Highlands Hiking Trail, managed by the Bureau of State Parks, and the North Country Trail, which stretches across a portion of western Pennsylvania on its way to Ohio.

How to Use This Guide

This book is meant to aid you in determining which trails you might most like to hike.

Each chapter identifies a hike by name, gives a brief summary of what it's like, and identifies its starting point, length, the approximate time needed to walk it, what the trail surface is like, and the relative difficulty. Also included is information about taking dogs on the hike, who else you might see on the trail, and in which seasons the hiking is best.

The books details as well who owns the land, when it's open, and who to contact for more information. You also get a map with each hike. They are tailored specifically to the hike directions; however, they are not meant to replace topographic maps, road maps, or the detailed maps you can sometimes get from land-managing agencies.

Finally, and perhaps most importantly, each chapter gives a detailed description of the hike, with turn-by-turn directions and information about what you might see along the way, be it wildlife, historical sights, rock formations, or interesting flowers and trees.

Trail Finder

Best Hikes for Water Lovers

1	Raccoon Creek State Park Wildflower Reserve
5	Todd Nature Reserve
8	Enlow Fork
9	Yough River Trail
10	Yellow Creek State Park—Damsite Trail
14	Quebec Run Wild Area
15	Ohiopyle State Park Ferncliff Peninsula
16	Flat Rock Trail
18	Laurel Hill State Park Loop

Best Hikes for Waterfalls

15	Ohiopyle State Park Ferncliff Peninsula
18	Laurel Hill State Park Loop

Best Hikes for Children

3	Bushy Run Battlefield—Edge Hill Trail
4	Frick Park
6	Jennings Environmental Education Center
16	Flat Rock Trail
18	Laurel Hill State Park Loop

Best Hikes for Dogs

3	Bushy Run Battlefield—Edge Hill Trail
4	Frick Park
7	Mingo Creek
16	Flat Rock Trail

Best Hikes for Great Views

10	Yellow Creek State Park—Damsite Trail
12	Mount Davis

Best Hikes for Picnics

Map Legend

═══⑤═══	Interstate Highway
──⑱──	State Highway
──3037──	Local Road
= = = = = =	Unpaved Road
▬▬▬▬▬	Featured Trail
- - - - - -	Trail
⊢−⊢−⊢−⊢	Railroad
〜〜〜	River/Creek
⬭	Lake
▦▦	Local & State Park & County/
▦▦	Natural Area/ Historic Site
▭	Bench
⛵	Boat Launch
‿	Bridge
•−•	Gate
✕	Mine/Quarry
🅿	Parking
🅿	Picnic Area
■	Point of Interest/Structure
◩	Shelter
⚲	Spring
≡	Steps
🚻	Restroom
○	Town
⓫	Trailhead
◪	Viewpoint/Overlook
≋	Visitor/Information Center
❷	Waterfall

1 Raccoon Creek State Park Wildflower Reserve

This hike, which begins and ends with hills but is relatively flat otherwise, winds through what is perhaps the most diverse habitat in Pennsylvania. Abundant wildflowers, rocky cliffs, and a picturesque stream are among the highlights.

Start: Raccoon Creek State Park Wildflower Reserve
Distance: 2.3-mile loop
Approximate hiking time: 1 to 1.5 hours
Difficulty: Easy to moderate, with two climbs broken up by lots of flat walking
Trail surface: Dirt paths
Seasons: Best between April and October
Other trail users: Birders
Canine compatibility: Dogs are prohibited in this area to protect its ecology.
Land status: State park
Fees and permits: None
Schedule: Open year-round

Maps: Trail map available by contacting Raccoon Creek State Park; USGS Aliquippa and USGS Hookstown.
Trail contacts: Raccoon Creek State Park, 3000 Route 18, Hookstown 15050-9416; (724) 899-2200; (724) 899-3611 for the Wildflower Reserve education center; www.dcnr.state.pa.us/stateparks/parks/raccooncreek.aspx
Special considerations: None of the trails here are marked with blazes, but they are generally easy to follow, and hikers are asked to stay on the trails.

Finding the trailhead: Take Interstate 279 south from Pittsburgh to U.S. Highway 22 east. Exit onto U.S. Highway 30 west. Travel about 9 miles along US 30 west and look for a sign on the right for the reserve. *DeLorme: Pennsylvania Atlas and Gazetteer:* Page 56 D2. GPS coordinates N40 30.424 / W80 21.824

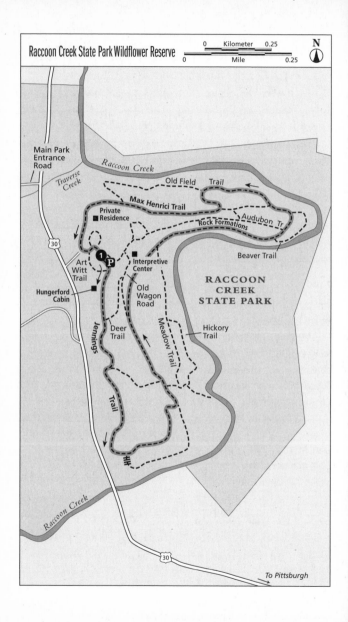

The Hike

Wildflowers like the trout lily, snow trillium, and harbinger-of-spring don't bloom at the same time as species like cone-flowers, asters, and ironweed. The first three sprout their colors in April, the latter three in August.

They all, though, flower eventually in one special place.

Raccoon Creek State Park's Wildflower Reserve is relatively small at just 314 acres. But it is unique. Botanists have recorded 756 plant species there—a similar-size patch of woods might more typically hold 200 to 300—so it's acre for acre perhaps the most diverse spot in Pennsylvania.

Credit for that goes to the reserve's variety of habitats: floodplains, reverting farms, hardwood forest, and pine plantations. This particular hike lets you explore each of those settings.

To begin, park in the lot near the interpretive center and follow Jennings Trail. This is the steepest part of the hike, climbing by pines and under oaks and hickories. You'll soon pass the Hungerford Cabin—once used by cartoonist Cy Hungerford, creator of World War II's Rosie the Riveter—on your right.

The trail then drops downhill to meet Deer Trail at mile 0.2. Continue right on Jennings. It parallels US 30 until turning away—and getting noticeably quieter—at mile 0.4. Stay to the left at a Y intersection with a set of steps, and you'll pass a bench before turning left again at a T intersection at mile 0.6.

Skirting the base of the hill, you'll find a junction with Meadow Trail at mile 0.7. Stay left until meeting Old Wagon Road, then turn right to remain on Jennings.

Bypass Meadow Trail when it comes in on the right again at mile 1.1, and you'll be rewarded with some wonderful scenery. The trail is squeezed between Raccoon Creek on the right and a tall, sheer wall of stone on the left.

The trail Ys yet again at mile 1.3. Ignore Beaver Trail to the right and go left until, at mile 1.6, you're at the junction of the Max Henrici and Old Field Trails. Turn right onto Old Field, into an area good for spotting late summer wildflowers.

Turn left at mile 1.8 onto a short connector path leading to Henrici Trail. Turn right onto Henrici, and you'll bypass a junction with Old Field Trail at mile 2.0. Soon—not long after the sound of traffic on Route 30 again reaches your ears—the trail bears left to climb uphill through a ravine bordered by tall pines.

That brings you to the driveway leading to the parking lot at mile 2.2. Turn left and return to the trailhead.

Miles and Directions

0.0 Start at the trailhead in the parking lot by the interpretive center.

0.1 Pass the Hungerford Cabin, named for a famous Pittsburgh newspaper editorial cartoonist, on your right.

0.2 Go right at the junction with Deer Trail.

0.5 Come to a bench along the trail. This is a good spot to take in the valley below.

0.7 Go left at the junction with Meadow Trail.

0.8 Turn right at the junction with Old Wagon Road.

1.1 Turn left at the junction with the Meadow Trail. You'll pass some rock cliffs on your left.

1.3 Turn left at the junction with Beaver Trail.

1.8 Go left at the junction with a connector trail leading to the Max Henrici Trail.

2.2 The trail meets a driveway here; turn left.

2.3 Arrive back at the parking area.

2 Beechwood Farms Nature Reserve

A relatively short hike through a nature preserve that contains just 134 acres, this loop is nonetheless enjoyable, especially if you want to stay close to Pittsburgh. You can join any walk here with one of Beechwood's many public nature programs or a trip to its store, too.

Start: Beechwood Farms Nature Center
Distance: 2.5-mile loop
Approximate hiking time: 1 to 2 hours
Difficulty: Easy to moderate, with just a few short hills
Trail surface: Dirt paths and lawn surfaces. Spring Hollow Trail is maintained as an "all peoples" trail, meaning that while it's not ADA compliant, it has been constructed to adhere to as many of those principles as possible, given the topography. It gets mulched every third year and averages 6 feet wide.
Seasons: Year-round
Other trail users: Cross-country skiers
Canine compatibility: Dogs are not permitted unless they are special-needs animals.
Land status: Owned by the

Western Pennsylvania Conservancy and leased to Audubon Society of Western Pennsylvania
Fees and permits: No fees or permits required
Schedule: Open year-round
Maps: Map available by contacting the Audubon Society of Western Pennsylvania; USGS Glenshaw.
Trail contacts: Audubon Society of Western Pennsylvania, 614 Dorseyville Road, Pittsburgh 15238; (412) 963-6100; www .aswp.org
Special considerations: Individual trails here are closed periodically in winter for the purposes of managing deer. Know, too, that while most of the reserve's trails are not blazed, they are marked at each intersection, so getting around is pretty simple.

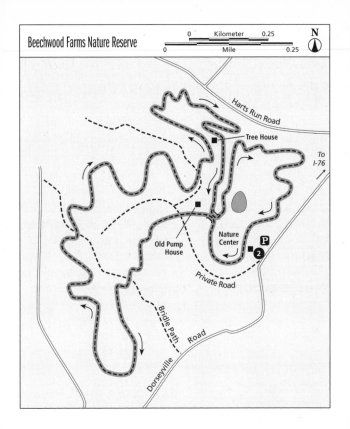

Finding the trailhead: From exit 48 of the Pennsylvania Turnpike, get onto Route 910/Yellow Belt. Turn left onto Locust Hill Road, go 1.4 miles, and turn right onto Guys Run Road, then turn right onto the Green Belt. After traveling 1.3 miles, go left onto Dorseyville Road and follow it to the nature reserve. *DeLorme: Pennsylvania Atlas and Gazetteer:* Page 57 D6. GPS coordinates N40 32.574 / W79 54.355

The Hike

A farmer in muddy boots and worn overalls would look out of place in Fox Chapel these days. It's one of Pittsburgh's most affluent communities.

A state senator by the name of William Flinn once ran a working farm here, though, and today 134 acres of what's left of it have been set aside as Beechwood Farms Nature Reserve. Managed by the Audubon Society of Western Pennsylvania, it offers 5 miles of hiking trails.

To start this hike, follow the sidewalk between the nature store and education building, then turn left and head uphill on Spring Hollow Trail. At mile 0.2, turn left, cross a private road, and follow Meadow View Trail. Cover another 0.1 mile and turn left onto Pine Hollow Trail. This is a good area for spotting white-tailed deer.

Cross a bridge and bridle trail at mile 0.5 and another at a pretty waterfall at mile 0.8. At mile 1.1, ignore a trail leading to the left that's blocked with brush and continue straight on Pine Hollow before taking the next left 100 feet or so farther on.

You'll come to an old pump house at mile 1.2. Turn left onto Meadow View. Re-cross the private road at mile 1.4, where you'll walk a short way through a field of goldenrod before turning left onto Woodland Trail, where the forest is thick with grapevines.

At mile 1.6, cross a small bridge and turn right onto Spring Hollow Trail, then right again onto Violet Trail. You'll pass a few benches on your way to the "tree house" at mile 1.8. Really a platform, it offers a panoramic view of the valley below, particularly when the leaves are off the trees.

At mile 1.9 you'll leave Spring Hollow by turning left onto Upper Fields Trail. Turn left at the next junction, at mile 2.1, onto Goldenrod Trail. You're back behind the nature center here.

The trail next takes you by a pond to a sign for Violet Trail. Follow Violet to mile 2.2, where another sign points TO WOODLAND. Turn right here. Walk to the bridge you crossed earlier, turn right, then at mile 2.3 turn left onto Oak Forest Trail. A few of the plants and trees in this area are identified with signs.

Cross a road at mile 2.4, heading back toward the pond. At the next junction, turn left to return to the nature center and your starting point.

Miles and Directions

- **0.0** Start this hike at the trailhead by the nature center, which has a gift shop that's worth visiting.
- **0.2** Turn left at the junction of Spring Hollow and Meadow View Trails. Note that a sign directs you to a vista a short ways off, if you're interested in a side hike.
- **0.5** The trail bisects a bridle trail. The woods open up here, so you'll see sky even if there are no horses.
- **0.8** The trail passes over a small waterfall. Taking a few steps off the trail gives you a good view of it.
- **1.2** Bypass an old pump house. If you peek inside, you can see some of the old machinery still in place.
- **1.8** The "Treetop" tree house, really an elevated platform extending out from the hillside, gives you a wonderful view of the valley below, especially when the leaves are off the trees.
- **2.1** The trail bypasses the pond study area. This is a good spot to see geese, frogs, and fish.
- **2.5** Return to the nature center and your vehicle.

3 Bushy Run Battlefield–Edge Hill Trail

Bushy Run Battlefield was the site of a key British victory over seven tribes of Indians in 1763. It was first memorialized in 1918, when the schoolchildren of Westmoreland County contributed one penny each—70,000 pennies in all—to buy six and a half acres and establish the battlefield as a park. Today, it's expanded to about 250 acres, and visitors can learn about its unique place in history by walking the Edge Hill Trail.

Start: Bushy Run Battlefield visitor center
Distance: 1.0-mile loop
Approximate hiking time: 30 minutes
Difficulty: Easy to moderate, with a few hills but wide, well-maintained trails
Trail surface: Dirt path
Seasons: Year-round
Other trail users: Cross-country skiers and mountain bikers
Canine compatibility: Dogs permitted, but they should be on a leash.
Land status: Pennsylvania Historical and Museum Commission land
Fees and permits: No fees or permits required
Schedule: Open year-round
Maps: Map available by contacting Bushy Run Battlefield; USGS Irwin and USGS Greensburg
Trail contacts: Bushy Run Battlefield, P.O. Box 468, Harrison City 15636-0468; (724) 527-5584; www.bushyrunbattlefield .com
Special considerations: The park is open to hiking every day year-round, but parking is limited to one lot at certain times. The visitor center is open from 9:00 a.m. to 5:00 p.m. Wednesday through Sunday from April 1 to October 31. There is an admission fee.

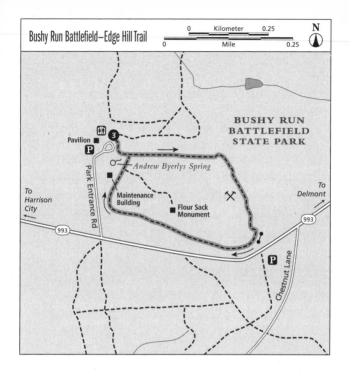

Bushy Run Battlefield–Edge Hill Trail

BUSHY RUN
BATTLEFIELD
STATE PARK

Pavilion

Park Entrance Rd

Andrew Byerlys Spring

Maintenance
Building

Flour Sack
Monument

To
Harrison
City

To
Delmont

Chestnut Lane

Finding the trailhead: Take U.S. Highway 22 east from Monroeville to Delmont. Exit onto Route 66 south. Turn right onto Route
993 west and go 3 miles to the park entrance. The trail begins by
the visitor center. *DeLorme: Pennsylvania Atlas and Gazetteer*: Page
72 B2. GPS coordinates N40 21.529 / W79 37.517

The Hike

There's no doubt the Battle of Bushy Run is historically sig-
nificant. By August of 1763, the Ottawa chief Pontiac and
his warriors had captured ten British forts, forced the aban-
donment of another, and had Forts Pitt and Detroit under

siege in what was the biggest Indian threat to the colonies in eighteenth-century America.

If Fort Pitt—which became Pittsburgh—fell, the "gateway to western expansion" would have been closed.

Then came the Battle of Bushy Run. Pontiac's forces temporarily ended their siege to attack British forces under the command of Col. Henry Bouquet. But Bouquet's troops, using tactics still studied by U.S. military officials, won a two-day battle and changed the course of history. You can learn a lot of that history by walking Edge Hill Trail.

Begin at the park's visitor center—worth a visit—and follow the stone steps downhill from its front doors. Cross over the Iroquois Nature Trail and go down wooden steps until the trail Ts. Turn left onto Edge Hill Trail.

You'll go only 100 feet or so before you see, on the right, a wooden post with a 1 on it. It's the first of nine markers that correspond with important features of the battle, this one representing the Native American position. A trail guide available at the visitor center explains everything.

The trail next winds under tall hemlocks and passes a bench on the left before turning uphill. Mile 0.5 brings you to marker 4 and another bench, this one facing a stone quarry carved out by settlers after the battle.

Just a little farther along, Edge Hill Trail angles right toward a stone wall and Route 993. Pass marker 5 and follow the trail into a field and to the Flour Sack monument. Notice how the pin oaks surrounding this field are planted in a semicircle; they represent the approximate position of British troops during the battle.

From the monument, walk toward the park's entrance road. When you come to marker 8—at mile 0.9—on the edge of the field, turn right and reenter the woods, keeping the maintenance building on your left. Mile 1.0 brings you to an old foundation and marker 9. This is the site of Andrew Byerly's Spring and, later, the Lewis Wanamaker farm.

From here, return up the steps to the visitor center to complete the loop.

Miles and Directions

0.0 Begin at the Bushy Run Battlefield visitor center. Interpretive and hands-on exhibits make this worth a visit before your hike.

0.2 A bench on the left, under some tall hemlocks, offers a shady rest spot. This is also a good spot from which to see deer and squirrels.

0.3 Bypass marker 3, which is on the right, next to a beech tree scarred by people who have carved their initials into the bark.

0.5 Pass a stone quarry that dates to the late 1700s on your right. Pioneers used the stone here in building homes and other structures.

0.9 Marker 8 stands on the edge of the field, beyond the Flour Sack monument.

1.0 Look on the left to see Andrew Byerly's Spring, marked by a sign and a stone foundation, then walk up a few steps to return to your car.

4 Frick Park

This loop hike through Frick Park involves only a few hills and will allow you to see the tiny Hot Dog Dam, an even smaller pond, and, if you're lucky, people playing lawn bowling at the only site in Pennsylvania where that game still goes on. Expect to see lots of people and dogs, too.

Start: The Frick Environmental Center

Distance: 5.1-mile loop

Approximate hiking time: 2.5 to 3 hours

Difficulty: Easy to moderate, with just a few climbs

Trail surface: Dirt paths

Seasons: Year-round

Other trail users: Cross-country skiers, bicyclists, and joggers

Canine compatibility: Dogs permitted, but they must be leashed outside of designated off-leash areas.

Land status: City park

Fees and permits: No fees or permits required

Schedule: Open year-round

Maps: Park map available by contacting Pittsburgh Parks and Recreation; USGS Pittsburgh East

Trail contacts: Pittsburgh Parks and Recreation, 414 Grant Street, Room 400, Pittsburgh 15219; (412) 255-2539; www .city.pittsburgh.pa.us/parks/index.html

Special considerations: Signs at the parking area warn you not to leave valuables in plain view on the seats of your car, as vandals have been a problem. If you're leaving something in your car, lock it in the trunk or hide it out of sight.

Finding the trailhead: From the Parkway West (Interstate 376), take exit 7 toward Edgewood/Swissvale. Turn right onto South Braddock Avenue, left onto Forbes Avenue, and left onto South Dallas Avenue. Finally, turn left onto Beechwood Boulevard. *DeLorme: Pennsylvania Atlas and Gazetteer:* Page 71 A6. GPS coordinates N40 26.172 / W79 54.408

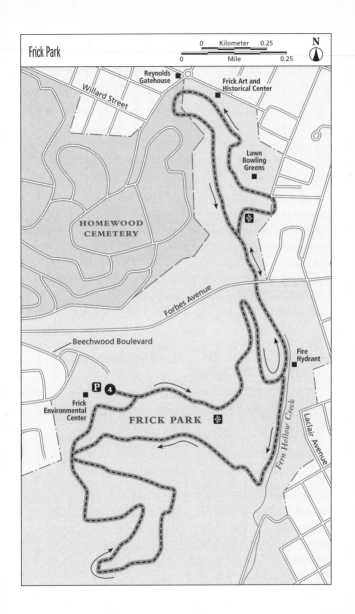

Frick Park

Willard Street

Reynolds
Gatehouse

Frick Art and
Historical Center

Lawn
Bowling
Greens

HOMEWOOD
CEMETERY

Forbes Avenue

Beechwood Boulevard

Fire
Hydrant

P 4

Frick
Environmental
Center

FRICK PARK

Fern Hollow Creek

Laclair Avenue

N

0   Kilometer   0.25

0   Mile   0.25

The Hike

Many hikes take you through areas of solitude. That's not the case here. Frick Park is always busy with a multicultural crowd of joggers, lawn bowlers, bicyclists, high school cross-country runners, and skiers.

This hike begins on the South Clayton Loop Trail near Frick Environmental Center. It's not marked, but if you walk to the end of the parking area, keeping the composting area and Meadow Trail on your left, you'll find it by a water fountain.

Walk a hundred yards or so and you'll pass the outdoor classroom and Nature Trail on your right. Bypass it for now.

Pass by an overlook at mile 0.4, and at mile 0.5 you'll make a sharp right turn and head downhill on Biddle Trail. You'll next come to a four-way intersection with a fire hydrant in the middle of the woods. Turn left onto Tranquil Trail, which parallels Fern Hollow Creek. Cross under Forbes Avenue and pass Hot Dog Dam on your right.

Mile 1.0 brings you to a Y; turn right onto Homewood Trail, which climbs to a nice view of the valley below. Just beyond a bench, make a sharp right onto Kensington Trail.

At a T intersection at mile 1.2, make a 90-degree turn left onto Hawthorne Trail. You'll pass the lawn bowling club and Frick Art and Historical Center.

Continue past steps on the left to the Gatehouse at Reynolds Street and then turn left onto Tranquil Trail near a cemetery at mile 1.6. Follow Tranquil back past the turnoff for Homewood Trail and the intersection with Biddle Trail.

You'll turn right onto Falls Ravine Trail at mile 2.8 by a pavilion and go uphill past rock formations. Make a sharp left at mile 3.2 onto Lower Riverview Trail.

Pass a sign on the left for Firelane Extension, and at mile 3.9 you come to a Y. Turn right onto Riverview Trail. This trail brings you to another Y at mile 4.6. To the left is a leash-free area for dog owners. Instead, turn right and go downhill on Riverview Extension.

Mile 4.8 brings you back to where you first turned onto Lower Riverview. This time, turn left onto Ravine Trail and circle a gully until you come to a junction with Nature Trail at mile 4.9. Turn right onto Nature Trail and, in another 0.1 mile, meet South Clayton Loop. Turn left and walk back to the parking lot.

Miles and Directions

0.0   Begin this hike at the South Clayton Loop trailhead, near a water fountain.

0.4   On the right, at a section of split-rail fence, there is an overlook that presents a nice view, especially when the leaves are off the trees.

1.0   Turn right at the junction with Homewood Trail, which leads to a bench at another nice overlook.

1.5   Look on the right for the fields used by the Frick Park Lawn Bowling Club. This is the only place in the state where this sport is still regularly played.

2.8   Turn right at a junction with Falls Ravine Trail. A pavilion here makes a nice place to stop and take a break on a hot day.

3.2   Turn left at a junction with Lower Riverview Trail.

3.9   Turn right at a junction with Riverview Trail.

4.6   Here you come to a junction with Riverview Extension; turn right.

4.9   Look on the left to see a platform that hosts many of the programs put on at the outdoor classroom.

5.1   Arrive back at the parking lot.

5 Todd Nature Reserve

Todd Nature Reserve is the older—if lesser well known—of two properties owned by the Audubon Society of Western Pennsylvania. This hike through the 176-acre woodland lets you experience streams shaded by dark hemlocks, boulder fields, and a pond banked by regenerating forest.

Start: Todd Nature Reserve parking lot
Distance: 1.1-mile loop
Approximate hiking time: 0.5 to 1 hour
Difficulty: Easy, with just two short climbs along several level, well-maintained trails
Trail surface: Dirt paths
Seasons: Year-round
Other trail users: Birders
Canine compatibility: Dogs prohibited, except for special-needs animals
Land status: Audubon Society of Western Pennsylvania

Fees and permits: No fees or permits required
Schedule: Open year-round
Maps: Map available by contacting the Audubon Society of Western Pennsylvania; USGS Freeport.
Trail contacts: Audubon Society of Western Pennsylvania, 614 Dorseyville Road, Pittsburgh 15238; (412) 963-6100; www .aswp.org
Special considerations: This area is closed during the state's two-week firearms deer season, which begins the Monday after Thanksgiving, so that hunters can help control deer.

Finding the trailhead: From Pittsburgh, take Route 28 north to exit 17. Take Route 356 north for 0.8 mile to a right turn onto Monroe Road. Go 1.2 miles and, at a fork in the road, turn right onto Kepple Road. Go 1.8 miles and look for the parking lot on the right. *DeLorme: Pennsylvania Atlas and Gazetteer:* Page 58 C1. GPS coordinates N40 43.973 / W79 42.116

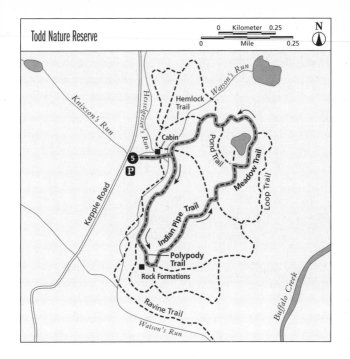

Todd Nature Reserve

Knixson's Run

Hesselgesser's Run

Watson's Run

Hemlock Trail

Cabin

Pond Trail

Meadow Trail

Loop Trail

5

P

Kepple Road

Indian Pipe Trail

Polypody Trail

Rock Formations

Ravine Trail

Watson's Run

Buffalo Creek

0   Kilometer   0.25
0   Mile   0.25

N

The Hike

Military battles can change history, as can earthquakes, plagues, and inventions.

So, too, can the tiniest ripples, as the existence of Todd Nature Reserve attests.

In the 1880s, a teenage W. E. Clyde Todd was studying birds on his grandparents' farm near Sarver. He spotted a nesting magnolia warbler. The discovery had significance; previously, no one realized the birds nested so far south.

Still, that might have become only a dusty footnote in history except that it spurred Todd to a noteworthy career in ornithology and, later, to donate land for the creation of Todd Nature Reserve. Now, new generations can enjoy nature there—all thanks to one teen's glimpse of a far-flying bird.

To take this hike, begin at the parking lot off Kepple Road. A sign on the left marks the trailhead.

Go down a few steps and turn right onto a service road. It parallels Knixon's Run and Ys in less than 100 yards. Straight ahead is Ravine Trail. Instead, turn left and cross a bridge to a cabin, site of nature programs and a visitor's log.

Next, walk to an adjacent clearing and follow the red-blazed Loop Trail. It winds beneath hemlocks until taking you to a junction with Indian Pipe Trail at mile 0.1. Turn right to stay on Loop Trail.

At mile 0.4, turn left and go uphill on the orange-blazed Polypody Trail, named for a small fern that grows on the boulders here. You'll wind around and between rocks larger than SUVs.

Shortly the trail bisects white-blazed Indian Pipe Trail, named for a whitish pipelike plant that blooms in July. Turn left onto Indian Pipe and walk until, at mile 0.6, you see a sign for Meadow Trail. It's not on the map, but turn right and follow it until it joins Pond Trail at mile 0.7.

Turn right onto Pond; at a Y on the far side, turn left to rejoin Loop Trail. Make a right to stay on Loop at mile 0.9, then turn left again onto Indian Pipe at a sign. Pass Hemlock Trail on the right, turn right onto Loop Trail again at mile 1.0, and come to another, larger bridge at mile 1.1. Cross it and you are back at the cabin. Descend its steps and retrace your path to the trailhead.

Miles and Directions

0.0   Begin at the parking lot. There is not a lot of space here, but except for the busiest weekends, that's not usually a problem.

0.1   After crossing a small bridge, you'll come to a junction with Indian Pipe Trail. Turn right and follow Loop Trail.

0.4   Turn left onto Polypody Trail and look for the small ferns that give it its name.

0.7   The trail brings you to the edge of a pond. There's a bench here in case you want to stop and look for waterfowl, frogs, or deer.

0.9   After you've circled the pond, the trail meets Loop Trail. Turn right onto Loop, heading toward some hemlocks.

1.0   Bypass a sign on the right for Hemlock Trail and continue straight (unless you want to spend a few minutes in the shade on a hot afternoon).

1.1   Cross one last bridge and head right, uphill, to go past the cabin again and retrace your steps to the parking lot, which is about 100 yards farther along.

6 Jennings Environmental Education Center

This is a fairly easy hike—it has just one challenging climb—and can be combined with one of Jennings Environmental Education Center's many nature programs for a full day of fun outdoors. Programs typically cover everything from tree identification and wildflowers to rattlesnakes and Native American culture, with some specifically for children.

Start: The visitor parking lot near the entrance to the park's prairie
Distance: 3.0-mile loop
Approximate hiking time: 2 hours
Difficulty: Easy to moderate, due to flat terrain
Trail surface: Dirt paths
Seasons: Year-round, but this hike is especially good in late July or early August, when the park's prairie is in full bloom.
Other trail users: Skiers and snowshoers
Canine compatibility: Dogs permitted, but they must be on a leash
Land status: State park
Fees and permits: No fees or permits required

Schedule: Open year-round. Check with the park for a calendar of events and a program schedule.
Maps: Map available by contacting Jennings Environmental Education Center; USGS Slippery Rock
Trail contacts: Jennings Environmental Education Center, 2951 Prospect Road, Slippery Rock 16057-8701; (724) 794-6011; www.dcnr.state.pa.us/stateparks/parks/jennings.aspx
Special considerations: If you walk your dog through Jennings' prairie—which is also home to endangered massasauga rattlesnakes—be sure to keep your pet on a leash so that neither he nor the snakes get hurt.

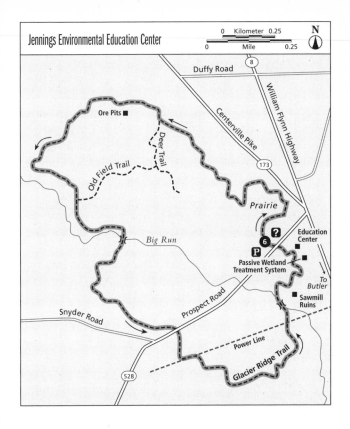

Finding the trailhead: Jennings Environmental Education Center is located near Slippery Rock. Take the Pennsylvania Turnpike to exit 39 (Butler), then follow Route 8 north for about 31 miles. Turn left onto Route 528, known locally as Prospect Road. *DeLorme: Pennsylvania Atlas and Gazetteer:* Page 43 D5. GPS coordinates N41 00.593 / W80 00.287

The Hike

The eastern massasauga is an unusual creature by Pennsylvania standards, so it's fitting that it survives best in a place that's equally unique.

The massasauga is one of three rattlesnake species in Pennsylvania; it's also the smallest and rarest. Endangered by state standards, they're hanging on where old meadows with low-lying wet spots abut higher, drier ground.

Jennings Environmental Education Center, site of the state's only publicly owned relict prairie—the little piece of prairie that remains in the midst of a forest ecosystem—has just that habitat, so it's home to snakes and some truly unusual wildflowers.

To begin, park in the lot adjacent to the prairie. Follow the path and, in less than 200 feet, continue straight past a sign for the Blazing Star Trail. At mile 0.1, turn right onto the Prairie Loop Trail, where interpretive signs explain what you're looking at.

At mile 0.4, turn right onto Blazing Star Trail, then make another right onto Deer Trail. Turn right onto Oak Woods Trail at mile 0.6. Cross a bridge at mile 1.1, climb a short hill, and, at mile 1.4, head downhill. At mile 1.5, turn right and cross a bridge onto Hepatica Trail.

You'll come to a Y at mile 1.7. Turn right onto Glacier Ridge Trail, which crosses Route 528 and enters Moraine State Park. Ignore the black blazes as you trek steeply uphill.

The trail crosses a power line at mile 1.8 and splits. Turn left onto the North Country Trail, marked by blue blazes, and then, at mile 1.9, turn right and uphill onto Ridge Trail.

Continue on Ridge, ignoring a trail on the right leading to a campground, and wind back to the power line. At mile 2.2, turn left onto Black Cherry Trail. Continue past bridges on the left at miles 2.3 and 2.5 until you're ultimately following a small stream tinted orange by acid mine drainage.

At mile 2.6, turn left and cross a bridge onto Old Mill Trail, past the ruins of an old sawmill. Continue to a series of ponds that serve as a passive mine drainage treatment system.

Circle the ponds counterclockwise to wind up at a shelter with signs explaining how the system works. Next, jump onto Wood Whisperer Trail, heading toward the park education center. At mile 2.7, turn left when the trail Ts and follow it along the center's observation deck.

Continue behind the building until you see a sign pointing to the prairie area trails where you parked.

Miles and Directions

0.0 Start this hike at the trailhead located at the entrance to the park's prairie area.

0.1 Turn right at the junction with the Prairie Loop Trail to begin your walk around the unique habitat.

0.6 Turn right again at the junction with Oak Woods Trail. Take a few steps and then look to the left to see a deer exclosure, a section of woods fenced to keep hungry deer out long enough for the preferred tree species like oak to regenerate.

1.1 A couple of stumps, cut to serve as chairs, complete with backs, make a nice resting spot.

1.7 You'll come to a juncture with Glacier Ridge Trail, which leads to Moraine State Park. It is home to several nice hikes, too.

1.8 Cross a power line, being alert for white-tailed deer. They often feed on the line's edges early and late in the day.

2.6 Look on the right for the ruins of an old sawmill.

2.7 The trail brings you to a shelter with signs explaining how the passive acid mine drainage treatment system in place works. It's a reminder how the steel industry that boomed in downtown Pittsburgh—relying on coal and coke—impacted all of the surrounding countryside.

3.0 Return to the parking area, but only after taking time to visit the interpretive center first.

7 Mingo Creek

Mingo Creek County Park southwest of Pittsburgh is a true multiuse park, popular with everyone from horseback riders and picnickers to history buffs and model airplane operators. There's plenty for hikers to like, too, though, in the way of scenery and wildlife.

Start: Ebeneezer Bridge/picnic shelter #4

Distance: 3.1-mile loop

Approximate hiking time: 1.5 to 2 hours

Difficulty: Easy to moderate, with a few climbs

Trail surface: Dirt paths, gravel and paved roads, and a paved biking trail

Seasons: Year-round

Other trail users: Horseback riders and mountain bikers

Canine compatibility: Dogs permitted, but they should be leashed.

Land status: County park

Fees and permits: No fees or permits required

Schedule: Open from dawn to dusk year-round

Maps: Trail map available by contacting Washington County Parks and Recreation; USGS Hackett

Trail contacts: Washington County Parks and Recreation, Courthouse Square, 100 West Beau Street, Suite 101, Washington 15301; (724) 228-6867; www.co.washington.pa.us/main department.aspx?menuDept=21

Special considerations: Located in rural Washington County, Mingo Creek County Park sees a lot of horseback riders, and a portion of this hike shares a route open to them. It can be hiked at any time, but it's best in dry weather. When it's been wet and muddy, that horse traffic can create ruts.

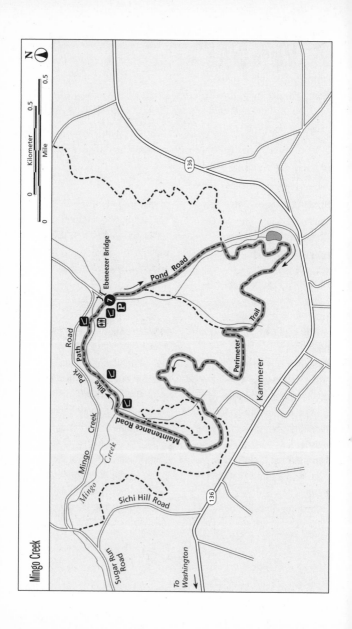

Finding the trailhead: From Pittsburgh, take Interstate 79 south to exit 43 (Houston/Eighty-Four). Turn right onto Route 519 south, then turn left onto Route 136 east. Go about 6 miles and turn left onto Sichi Hill Road. Turn right at the stop sign at the bottom of the hill, then take the next right into the park. *DeLorme: Pennsylvania Atlas and Gazetteer:* Page 71 C5. GPS coordinates N40 11.503 / W80 02.431

The Hike

It wouldn't be fair, or even accurate, to say that no one knows about Mingo Creek Park. It attracts trout anglers each spring, hosts high school graduation parties each summer, and draws visitors to see its covered bridges each fall. But it's not known as a hiking mecca either.

That's too bad. Tucked away in the rolling, pastoral hills of Washington County, Mingo Creek is a beautiful park, home to varied habitats and wildlife. This hike allows you to experience that without having to tackle any especially rugged country.

To begin, park by picnic shelter #4 and the covered Ebeneezer Bridge. Hike up Pond Road, a gravel maintenance road closed to vehicle traffic.

In a little less than 0.1 mile, a side trail branches off to the right. Ignore it and continue straight until you see orange blazes—marking Perimeter Trail—at mile 0.4.

Turn right and enter the woods on this path. It climbs steadily through young forest thick with grapevines until cresting a ridge at mile 0.6. As you start down the other side, notice an ancient beech tree and several mammoth oaks. They're magnificent in their antiquity, wise old kings whose reign dates to long-ago days when this wood was a pasture, as weathered fence posts here attest.

The trail next zigzags downhill until coming to a T at a trickle of a stream at mile 0.9; turn left. Keep alert for white-tailed deer here.

Follow the orange blazes as the trail passes a gas line and crosses several gullies. The trail then loops around and, at mile 1.3, enters a stand of tall Austrian pines. Meadows border the trail on the left starting at mile 1.7. This is another good spot to encounter deer, as well as turkeys.

When you reach mile 2.0, the trail meets a paved maintenance road. Turn right and follow the road downhill past a sign for Old Spring Trail, a parking lot, and a playground.

Just after crossing a bridge over Mingo Creek, at mile 2.6, turn right onto the paved walking/bike trail. It parallels Mingo Creek, buffered by tall sycamores in places.

The path continues on, passing restrooms, shelters, and benches that make nice resting points before re-crossing Mingo Creek to wind up at the lot where you began.

Miles and Directions

0.0 Start this hike by picnic shelter #4 and Ebeneezer Bridge, one of many covered bridges in Washington County. There are so many, in fact, that a festival to celebrate them is held each fall.

0.1 Bypass a side trail that branches off to the right.

0.4 Turn right at the junction with Perimeter Trail, which is open to horseback riding and often marked by hoofprints.

0.6 Enter an old-growth forest, remarkable for some of the very large specimens to be found right at the trail's edge.

0.9 The trail Ts at a small stream, which can be dry in summer. Ignore the seemingly more obvious trail to the right and instead go left.

1.3 After climbing a hill, the trail enters a large stand of Austrian pines.

1.7 Look for a series of meadows on the left. These are good places to spot deer and turkeys. In April and May you might even be lucky enough to see a turkey gobbler strutting, tail fanned out wide, in an annual courtship display.

2.0 The trail meets with a paved maintenance road. Turn right and follow the road downhill.

2.6 Turn right onto the walking/biking trail just after crossing a bridge over Mingo Creek. The creek gets stocked with trout each year for the fishing season that begins in mid-April, so expect to see lots of anglers along the banks at that time of year.

3.1 Return to the starting point, perhaps to wind up with a picnic lunch.

8 Enlow Fork

This is a relatively easy hike along a gated road on State Game Lands 302 on the border of Greene and Washington Counties. It largely follows the Enlow Fork of Wheeling Creek and is rich in wildflowers, birds, and wildlife. It's a good winter trail, too.

Start: The parking lot on a gravel road leading to the game lands
Distance: 6.8 miles out-and-back
Approximate hiking time: 3 to 3.5 hours
Difficulty: Easy, due to flat terrain
Trail surface: Gated gravel and dirt road
Seasons: Year-round
Other trail users: Hunters, bicyclists, and cross-country skiers
Canine compatibility: Dogs permitted
Land status: State game lands
Fees and permits: No fees or permits required
Schedule: The game land is open year-round, but this land was bought and is maintained using money from the sale of hunting licenses, so hunters have first use of the land. If you're

planning to come here with an organized group, you need approval from the Pennsylvania Game Commission beforehand, particularly at certain times of year.
Maps: Map of State Game Lands 302 available by contacting the Pennsylvania Game Commission; USGS Wind Ridge
Trail contacts: Pennsylvania Game Commission, Southwest Region Office, 4820 Route 711, Bolivar 15923; (724) 238-9523; www.pgc.state.pa.us
Special considerations: This area is very popular with hunters, primarily from October through late January and again from late April to late May. If you want to hike here at those times of year, it's best to do so on Sunday, when most hunting is prohibited.

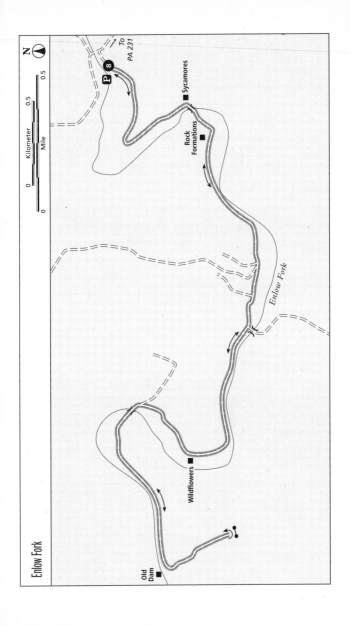

Enlow Fork

N

Kilometer
0   0.5
0   0.5
Mile

To
PA 231

P 8

Sycamores

Rock
Formations

Enlow Fork

Wildflowers

Old
Dam

Finding the trailhead: Get off Interstate 70 at the Claysville exit and turn east onto U.S. Highway 40. Go 0.9 mile, then turn south onto Route 231. Go 3.5 miles, bear right when the road starts downhill, and continue 7.9 miles to a junction in West Finley. Turn left onto Route 3037, go 2.4 miles, and turn right over an iron bridge. Go uphill on this gravel road for 1.7 miles and then turn sharply right at a state game lands sign. Follow the road to the end and park at the gate. *DeLorme: Pennsylvania Atlas and Gazetteer:* Page 84 A2. GPS coordinates N39 57.625 / W80 27.803

The Hike

Of all the trees that grow in Pennsylvania, one of the most unique is the mighty sycamore. Their trunks are a desert camouflage pattern of brown, beige, yellow, pale green, and white. Their bark peels off in long, flat sheets, almost like primitive pieces of paper. And massive? These trees probably average 70 to 100 feet in height in most places, with trunks that are 3 feet around. But specimens have been known to live for five centuries and stretch more than a dozen feet across at the base.

You won't see any quite that big on Game Lands 302, but they are one of the interesting features here.

Start your hike at the parking area at the end of the gravel entrance road. Go around a gate at the left side of the parking lot.

You'll walk uphill, keeping a large meadow on your right, then turn sharply left to follow the road at mile 0.2. Mile 0.4 brings you to an iron bridge over Enlow Fork. You'll see wildflowers here, as well as the first of many sycamores. Squirrels are common, too, as are chipmunks, great blue herons, belted kingfishers, and wood ducks, which nest in hollow sycamores whenever they can.

The road passes a few interesting rock formations until unmarked roads come in from the right at miles 1.6 and 1.7. Ignore them and continue along the main road. You'll come to another iron bridge on the left at mile 1.9. Part of its decking is gone, but you can cross it if you want to take a side trip or peek into the stream below. Otherwise, continue straight on the main road.

Mile 2.2 brings you to an area that often holds a variety of wildflowers, including common yarrow, orange touch-me-not, pokeweed, great blue lobelia, and wingstem.

Ignore another road that comes in from the right at mile 2.5 and you'll come to a third bridge at mile 2.6. Watch here for buckeye trees, relatively common on this extreme western edge of the state but scarce elsewhere.

Just before reaching a gate at mile 3.4, which marks the end of the hike in this direction, the road turns sharply left. Look straight ahead before making the turn and you can see an old dam. At the gate, turn around and retrace your steps to your vehicle.

Miles and Directions

0.0 Start at the parking area that really is only a wide spot at the end of the road.

0.4 The trail crosses Enlow Fork using an iron bridge. If you stop halfway across and peer into the water, you'll often see fish.

0.6 Look on the right for some interesting rock formations.

1.7 There are a number of sycamores in this area, but here stands one of the most impressive.

1.9 To the left, off the trail, sits another iron bridge.

2.2 The floodplain between the trail and Enlow Fork holds many wildflowers in this area.

2.6 Cross one more iron bridge, being sure to look for the buckeye trees that grow in the woods in this area. You can recognize them by their spiky, ball-shaped fruit.

3.4 A gate here marks the end of the hike in this direction. Just before reaching this gate, look for the old dam that sits nearby.

6.8 Return to the parking area where you started.

9 Yough River Trail

The Yough River Trail is part of the Great Allegheny Passage, a 150-mile rail trail connecting Pittsburgh with Cumberland, Maryland, though a connection to the C&O Canal path will let you go 316 miles and all the way to Washington, D.C. This particular section of trail follows the path of what was a Pittsburgh & Lake Erie Railroad line. It's a perfectly flat walk over crushed stone.

Start: The Arthur H. King II access area in West Newton
Distance: 6.0 miles one way
Approximate hiking time: 4 to 5 hours
Difficulty: Easy, as it's flat and wide
Trail surface: Crushed limestone
Seasons: Year-round
Other trail users: Bicyclists, cross-country skiers, joggers, snowshoers, and horseback riders
Canine compatibility: Dogs permitted, but they must be leashed.

Land status: Rail trail
Fees and permits: No fees or permits required
Schedule: Open year-round
Maps: Map available by contacting the Regional Trail Corporation; USGS Donora
Trail contacts: Regional Trail Corporation, 111 Collinsburg Road, West Newton 15089; (724) 872-5586; www.youghrivertrail.com
Special considerations: This rail trail is generally in the open, without shade, so be prepared for lots of sun.

Finding the trailhead: From Interstate 70, take exit 51B to Route 31 west and then turn onto Route 136 toward West Newton. Cross a bridge over the Yough River and make an immediate left into the parking lot. *DeLorme: Pennsylvania Atlas and Gazetteer:* Page 71 C7. GPS coordinates N40 12.668 / W79 46.214

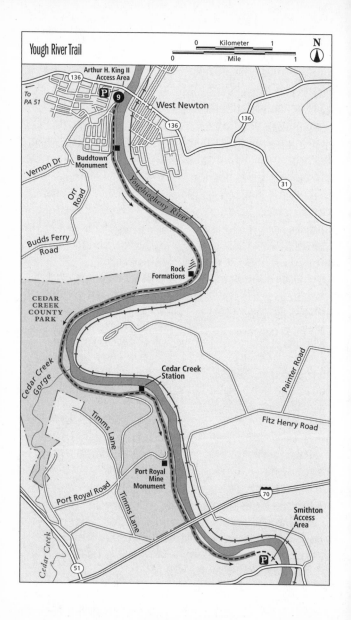

The Hike

June 10, 1901, was a day of tragedy for those connected to Port Royal Mine No. 2. On that day at that mine in West Newton, an underground explosion large enough to shock even miners numbed to constant danger occurred. The disaster attracted national attention for claiming the lives of more than twenty miners and would-be rescuers, according to newspapers covering the incident at the time.

Today, a monument to those lost souls exists along the Yough River Trail, a rail trail that covers 43 miles in its northern section. To hike this 6-mile portion, start at the Arthur H. King II access in West Newton and turn right, or upstream, to head south along the trail.

You'll pass the first of several benches at mile 0.5. Go around a gate at mile 0.7, where there's a monument on the left explaining the history of Buddtown.

You'll pass beneath a power line at mile 1.0 and over a road at mile 1.5. Deer tracks are common here, and fox squirrels are plentiful, too.

Soon, the hillside rises almost vertically from the trail on your right. Water trickles over these bluffs in numerous places, creating mini waterfalls in summer and daggerlike stalactites of opaque ice in winter.

Mile 3.1 brings you to Cedar Creek Gorge, the most beautiful section of trail. Here, by a bridge, you'll find a side path worthy of exploration, particularly when spring's wildflowers are in bloom.

Another 0.2 mile brings you to Cedar Creek Station, a refreshments stand and bike rental on the left side of the trail, in Cedar Creek County Park. The station is open from April to October, but you can use a restroom or picnic year-round. There's even space to camp, if you reserve a site ahead of time. All of that makes this is a nice ending spot if you want to shorten this hike a bit.

Otherwise, continue on until, at mile 4.6, you come to Saw Mill Run and the marker for the Port Royal Mine disaster. The I-70 bridge at mile 5.6 is the next landmark. Continue following the trail to the parking area in Smithton at mile 6.0.

Pick up your second car here if you're doing a shuttle hike, or turn and hike back.

Miles and Directions

0.0 Begin at the Arthur H. King II access area, which offers ample parking.

0.5 A bench offers a nice spot to stop and look over the river.

0.7 Buddtown Historical Marker, on the left, gives you a glimpse into the area's past.

1.5 The trail crosses over a road near some property posted against trespassing.

3.1 Here, at Cedar Creek Gorge, is a great spot to look for spring wildflowers. You'll likely see some tiny waterfalls, too, if it's been especially rainy.

3.3 Cedar Creek Station, with its picnic tables, restrooms, and, in season, concession stand, is a pleasant place to stop and just watch the river roll by.

4.6 Pass a historical marker explaining the Port Royal Mine disaster on the right.

5.6 The trail passes under the I-70 bridge.

6.0 Arrive at the Smithton access area. A "beach" here, where the river is lazy and slow, has long been a favorite swimming hole for locals.

10 Yellow Creek State Park—Damsite Trail

Since its dedication on July 4, 1976, Yellow Creek State Park has become immensely popular with picnickers, swimmers, boaters, and anglers. Hikers haven't always viewed it with the same level of desire, though. That's too bad because the park has several nice trails, perhaps the best being Damsite Trail. It's been rerouted—it's longer and shaped differently than the park map would have you believe—but is a beautiful hike nonetheless.

Start: Parking area at the end of Hoffman Road (Township Road 762)

Distance: 3.0-mile loop

Approximate hiking time: 1.5 to 2 hours

Difficulty: Easy to moderate, with few hills and at least half of the hike along a wide, flat service road

Trail surface: Dirt path

Seasons: Year-round

Other trail users: Cross-country skiers, mountain bikers, anglers, and hunters

Canine compatibility: Dogs permitted, but they must be on a leash

Land status: State park

Fees and permits: No fees or permits required

Schedule: Open year-round

Maps: Map available by contacting Yellow Creek State Park; USGS Brush Valley

Trail contacts: Yellow Creek State Park, 170 Route 259 Highway, Penn Run 15765-5941; (724) 357-7913; www.dcnr .state.pa.us/stateparks/parks/ yellowcreek.aspx

Special considerations: The dam overlook features some very high, very steep drop-offs. There is some fencing in place, but there are lots of opportunities to fall and be seriously hurt if you get careless, too. Use extreme caution, especially with children.

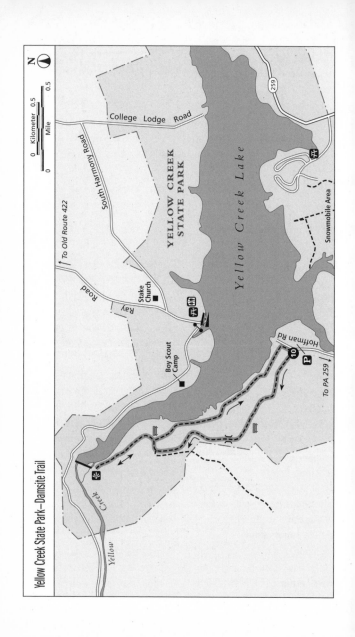

Yellow Creek State Park–Damsite Trail

Finding the trailhead: From U.S. Highway 22 east from Monroeville, turn right onto U.S. Highway 119 north just east of Blairsville. Turn right onto Route 56 east, then left onto Route 259 north. Turn left onto Hoffman Road (Township Road 762) and follow it to a parking lot by a gate at a dead end. *DeLorme: Pennsylvania Atlas and Gazetteer.* Page 59 D6. GPS coordinates N40 34.315 / W79 02.409

The Hike

Yellow Creek State Park is one of those places that came to be because of a desire to take the outdoors to the people.

In 1964 the Project 70 Land Acquisition and Borrowing Act was signed into law, authorizing the state to spend $70 million to, among other things, put a state park within 25 miles of every resident of Pennsylvania. Yellow Creek was one of the results.

This hike lets you explore a portion of the park with a "big woods" feel to it.

To begin, park at the end of Hoffman Road, where a sign marks the trailhead. The trail follows the crest of a hill, with red pines on your right, and Ys at mile 0.2; stay left to avoid a brushy detour. Next, just beyond a signpost at mile 0.4, you'll find a bench. All around, ground pine—a vine that looks like a Lilliputian forest—provides green color even in the depths of winter.

The trail winds downhill and Ys again at mile 0.5. Bear left at a sign and follow the red blazes. You'll cross a bridge at mile 0.6 and another a few steps farther along, with a bench just a bit beyond that.

The most challenging part of the hike comes next. Shortly after passing the mile 0.8 marker, climb uphill through an open woods. If you stop to catch your breath, some nice views of the lake are visible on the right.

Cross another bridge at mile 1.0 and, at a post for mile 1.2 (though it seemed less than that when measured on a GPS), bear left. A few feet farther on, you come to an intersection. A road goes to the left, and a few red blazes, leftover markers from before the trail was rerouted, are visible straight ahead. Ignore both and turn right—as a sign indicates—to go downhill toward a bench. At this T, turn left again.

The trail follows a service road that slopes downhill before ultimately, at mile 1.4, bringing you to the dam overlook. The view here is gorgeous, so linger awhile.

When you're ready to go, retrace your steps until you come to the bench you passed earlier. Turning right would take you back the way you came; instead, go straight, following the signs for the trailhead. The trail here can be soggy and wet in spots, as you're near the lakeshore, but it's very pretty.

Mile 2.9 brings you to a T intersection with Hoffman Road, which disappears into Yellow Creek Lake on the left. Turn right and walk uphill to the gate where you parked to complete this loop.

Miles and Directions

0.0 Begin at the Hoffman Road parking area. The trail is on the opposite side of the road from the parking lot.

0.4 Here, at the first trail mileage marker, sits a bench. It offers a partial view of the lake when the leaves are off the trees.

0.6 The trail crosses a small stream over a bridge. The trail is usually no more than a trickle in midsummer but can be much higher in spring.

1.0 When the trail Ts, turn left on this wide path to go toward the dam.

1.4 Arrive at the Damsite overlook. If you've carried a fishing rod along, the stream below the dam offers some good—and largely untapped—fishing.

2.4 You'll come to the same stream that you crossed via a bridge earlier.

2.9 The trail Ts with Hoffman Road, which disappears into Yellow Creek Lake on the left. This is another good spot from which to fish, or just to sit and soak up the sun while watching boats go by.

3.0 Climb Hoffman Road to arrive back at the parking area. Unfortunately, there's often trash here, so consider doing yourself and others a favor by bagging some of it up and taking it out to a park dumpster.

11 Friendship Hill National Historic Site

This is an easy to moderate hike, with lots of wildlife—notably, white-tailed deer, gray and fox squirrels, and songbirds—to be seen. You get some nice views of the Monongahela River, too. What makes this hike really unique, however, is the opportunity to visit the Gallatin House, where you can get a guided tour, watch a video presentation, and learn about an important if little known American.

Start: The parking lot near the Gallatin House Visitor Center

Distance: 4.0-mile loop

Approximate hiking time: 2 hours

Difficulty: Easy to moderate, with a few climbs and descents

Trail surface: A short section of paved sidewalk, followed by dirt paths

Seasons: Year-round

Other trail users: Cross-country skiers in winter

Canine compatibility: Dogs permitted when leashed

Land status: National Park Service historic site

Fees and permits: No fees or permits required

Schedule: The site's trails are open year-round, but if you want to tour the Albert Gallatin House, you need to be there between 9:00 a.m. and 5:00 p.m. daily April through October. It's open Saturday and Sunday through winter.

Maps: Map available by contacting Friendship Hill National Historic Site; USGS Masontown

Trail contacts: Friendship Hill National Historic Site, 223 New Geneva Road, Point Marion 15474; (724) 725-9190; www.nps.gov/frhi

Special considerations: Hunting is not permitted on the site grounds, so this is a good place to hike on weekdays and Saturdays in the fall.

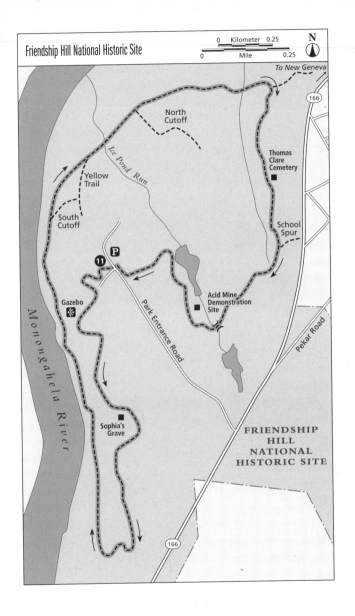

Friendship Hill National Historic Site

To New Geneva

166

North Cutoff

Ice Pond Run

Yellow Trail

South Cutoff

Thomas Clare Cemetery

School Spur

P

11

Gazebo

Park Entrance Road

Acid Mine Demonstration Site

Pekar Road

Monongahela River

Sophia's Grave

FRIENDSHIP HILL NATIONAL HISTORIC SITE

166

0   Kilometer   0.25

0   Mile   0.25

N

Finding the trailhead: Take U.S. Highway 119 south from Uniontown to Point Marion. Turn onto Route 166 north and go 3 miles to the park entrance. Follow the park road until you come to the parking lot for the visitor center. Park and start your hike here. *DeLorme: Pennsylvania Atlas and Gazetteer:* Page 85 B6. GPS coordinates N39 46.645 / W79 55.862

The Hike

Tragedy made Albert Gallatin an American hero of sorts. Born in Geneva, Switzerland, he traveled to America, ultimately settling on the banks of the Monongahela River. He called the area New Geneva and in 1789 laid plans to manufacture firearms, glass, and other items for fellow settlers.

Not long after he arrived, though, his wife died, changing the course of his life forever. He remarried, but his new bride wanted no part of living on the frontier, so Gallatin moved to the nation's capital. There, he served thirteen years as Secretary of the U.S. Treasury under presidents Jefferson and Madison, funding the Louisiana Purchase and the Lewis and Clark Expedition.

He always kept his original home, though, and today it's maintained by the National Park Service. You can stop by, learn a little history, then hike its grounds.

To begin, pass under the archway between the main Gallatin House and a later addition. At mile 0.2 you'll come to a gazebo and overlook of the river, known locally as the Mon.

Follow the green-blazed Main Loop Trail to a meadow and, at mile 0.3, turn right. You'll shortly reenter the woods and, at mile 0.4, come to Sophia's Grave, where Gallatin's first wife is buried.

Pass a small pond, cross a bridge, and, at mile 0.5, bypass the red-blazed Meadow Loop. You'll bypass the Meadow Loop again at mile 0.8, then descend steep steps toward the Monongahela. This is where you'll find the one eyesore along this hike: piles of tires dumped in the woods just past the site boundary.

You'll turn right to put the tires at your back and follow the Main Loop Trail as it parallels the river, where you might spot deer. The trail is wide and flat, offering easy walking.

Mile markers 1.9, 2.0, and 2.1 bring you to Ys in the trail; stay to the left each time. At mile 2.6 you come to a junction with the New Geneva Spur Trail. Turn right, almost doubling back, to follow the green-blazed Main Loop Trail.

At mile 2.8 you'll pass an interesting small cemetery, then at mile 3.1 bypass the School Spur.

At mile 3.3 you'll cross a bridge over Ice Pond Run, turn right onto the green-blazed Ice Pond Run Loop, and pass a marker explaining the impacts of acid mine drainage, visible as orange water here. At mile 3.8 you'll turn left into a field and walk its edge back to the entrance road. Turn right and return to the parking lot.

Miles and Directions

0.0 From the parking lot, follow the sidewalk to the Gallatin House, past a statue of Gallatin himself.

0.2 A gazebo offers a nice overlook of the Monongahela River.

0.4 Pass Sophia's Grave, which stands as a primitive-looking monument to the first love of Gallatin's life.

2.0 Cross Ice Pond Run, a small stream that's often dry in summer.

2.8 Look on the left for Clare Cemetery. Though often overgrown, it's worth a few minutes of your time.

3.3 Re-cross Ice Pond Run. Be sure to watch for white-tailed deer in this area.

3.8 Turn left at a junction with an open meadow. Deer are common here, too, as are fox and gray squirrels.

4.0 Turn right when the field meets the road to return to the parking area.

12 Mount Davis

Mount Davis is the highest point in Pennsylvania, 3,213 feet above sea level. Don't expect to see a singular majestic peak, however. The area around Mount Davis is one big plateau, so while you can get a very nice view from an observation tower, it's surprisingly flat.

Start: The Mt. Davis Picnic Area

Distance: 7.8-mile loop

Approximate hiking time: 3.5 to 4.5 hours

Difficulty: Moderate, with surprisingly few climbs but some areas of brushy trail

Trail surface: Dirt paths; gravel and grass roads

Seasons: Best between April and October

Other trail users: Cross-country skiers, hunters, snowmobilers, and, increasingly, mountain bikers

Canine compatibility: Dogs permitted

Land status: State forest

Fees and permits: No fees or permits required

Schedule: Open year-round

Maps: Trail map available by contacting Forbes State Forest; USGS Markleton

Trail contacts: Forbes State Forest, Bureau of Forestry, Forestry District #4, P.O. Box 519, Laughlintown 15655; (724) 238-1200; www.dcnr.state.pa.us/forestry/stateforests/forbes.aspx

Special considerations: This is the highest point of the state and is, appropriately enough, a place of extremes. Annual temperatures range from -30 degrees to 95 degrees Fahrenheit. It is not uncommon for winter snow depths to reach 3 to 4 feet—perhaps three times as deep as what you'll find at lower elevations. And frost has been observed at some point during every month of the year, too.

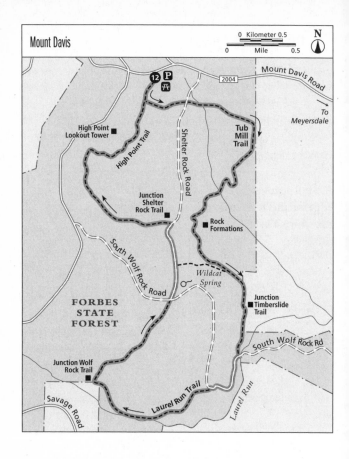

Finding the trailhead: Take the Pennsylvania Turnpike to the Somerset exit, then get onto Route 219 south. Go to Meyersdale, then follow Route 2004 to the picnic area. *DeLorme: Pennsylvania Atlas and Gazetteer*: Page 87 B5. GPS coordinates N39 47.612 / W79 10.093

The Hike

Mount Davis is the highest point in Pennsylvania, but you wouldn't know it. While it towers over the Ohio River valley to the west and the rich farm country to the east, it's just inches taller than some of the surrounding peaks.

Still, the greater Mt. Davis Natural Area and Forbes State Forest offer wonderful opportunities to enjoy the kind of nature common to southwestern Pennsylvania's mountains.

To begin, pick up High Point Trail near the western edge of the picnic area. Just past the 0.1-mile mark, turn left onto Tub Mill Trail, which winds through boulders and ferns.

At mile 0.5, cross Shelter Rock Road to stay on Tub Mill Trail. Keep your eyes open for blazes, as the trail is very narrow and can be hard to follow among the rocks and mountain laurel.

The trail climbs uphill at mile 1.7. You'll pass rock formations at mile 2.1, then come to large hemlocks and a small stream at mile 2.3. Tub Mill Trail stays near the stream, providing a cool, shaded walk.

At mile 2.5, near the state forest boundary, turn right and cross a small stream to stay on the trail. The junction with Timberslide Trail is just a couple of hundred yards farther ahead. Turn left to stay on Tub Mill.

Tub Mill Trail ends at South Wolf Rock Road at mile 2.9. Turn right and walk the road until, at mile 3.4, you can turn left onto Laurel Run Trail. Follow Laurel Run for 1.0 mile, then turn right onto Wolf Rock Trail.

At mile 5.2, cross directly over South Wolf Rock Road and enter the woods on Shelter Rock Road, a gated, grassy forest service road. Be sure, at a sign at mile 5.5, to check out Wildcat Spring, where water bubbles to the surface, constantly stirring gentle clouds of sand at the bottom of a pool.

Back on track, climb until mile 5.8, when you'll turn left onto Shelter Rock Trail. This will take you uphill through the heart of the Mt. Davis Natural Area, past laurel, ferns, and sassafras.

The payoff comes at mile 6.8, when you emerge at the Mt. Davis observation tower, which offers a splendid view of the country. Informational plaques offer interesting history, too.

When you're ready, follow High Point Trail as it winds first through a young forest and then through bigger timber closer to the picnic area. End the hike back where you started at mile 7.8.

Miles and Directions

0.0 Start this hike at the Mt. Davis Picnic Area.

0.1 Turn left at the junction with Tub Mill Trail. You'll wind up at this same spot on your way back out.

1.7 Climb uphill and cross a small stream.

2.1 The mountains that form the Laurel Highlands are famous, or infamous, for the rocks that sprout from the ground so often as to seem to outnumber the trees. You'll see some of the rock formations that are so common at this spot.

2.6 The trail comes to a junction with Timberslide Trail. Stay to the left to continue on Tub Mill Trail.

2.9 The trail empties onto the gravel South Wolf Rock Road. Turn right and climb uphill.

3.4 Turn left off of the road and back into the woods at the junction with Laurel Run Trail.

4.4 Turn right at a junction with Wolf Rock Trail.

5.5 At this point a sign on the right directs you to Wildcat Spring. It's worth stopping a moment to check out this small wonder.

5.8 Turn left at a junction with Shelter Rock Trail to follow the path, which narrows and becomes rocky again here.

6.8 Climb the observation tower to get a look at the mountains from Pennsylvania's highest point. The view can be stunning, especially in autumn when the fall foliage is blazing.

7.8 Return to the picnic area, which has a few pavilions and restrooms.

13 Laurel Mountain Loop

You'll be hiking at some high altitudes here—the trailhead lies at 2,708 feet—so expect to find snow and colder temperatures here when Pittsburgh is warmer and drier. Don't worry about having to do any climbing, though. Because this hike stays on the ridge the entire time, it offers flat walking.

Start: Across from the ski hut on Laurel Summit Road
Distance: 2.3-mile loop
Approximate hiking time: 1 to 1.5 hours
Difficulty: Easy to moderate, due to flat terrain, in warm weather. It can be more difficult in winter, sometimes to the point that snowshoes are necessary, as this area commonly has high levels of snow due to its geography and is typically 10 degrees colder than lower elevations, too.
Trail surface: Dirt paths
Seasons: Year-round
Other trail users: Cross-country skiers, snowshoers, mountain bikers, and hunters
Canine compatibility: Dogs permitted
Land status: State park and forest
Fees and permits: No fees or permits required
Schedule: Open year-round

Maps: Laurel Highlands Trail System map available by contacting Forbes State Forest; park map available by contacting Laurel Mountain State Park; USGS Ligonier and Bakersville
Trail contacts: Laurel Mountain State Park, c/o Linn Run State Park, P.O. Box 50, Rector 15677-0050; (724) 238-6623; www.dcnr.state.pa.us/stateparks/parks.laurelsummit.aspx; Forbes State Forest, Bureau of Forestry, Forestry District #4, P.O. Box 519, Laughlintown 15655; (724) 238-1200; www.dcnr.state.pa.us/forestry/stateforests/forbes.aspx
Special considerations: This area is very popular with cross-country skiers in the winter, so if you hike here then (and it's a good winter walk), trail etiquette calls for hikers and pets to stay out of established ski tracks.

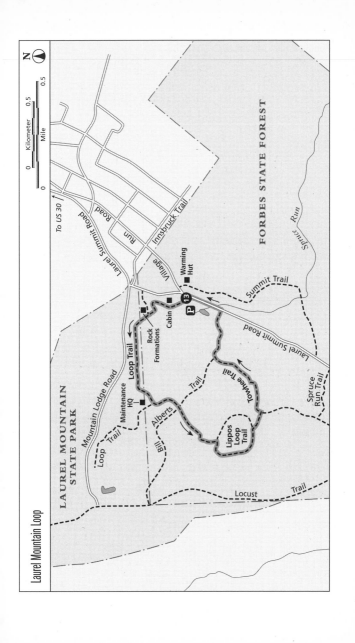

Laurel Mountain Loop

LAUREL MOUNTAIN STATE PARK

FORBES STATE FOREST

To US 30

Laurel Summit Road

Village Run

Innsbruck Trail

Warming Hut

Summit Trail

Cabin

Rock Formations

P 13

Spruce Run

Laurel Summit Road

Mountain Lodge Road

Loop Trail

Maintenance HQ

Bill Alberts Trail

Towhee Trail

Lippos Loop Trail

Spruce Run Trail

Loop Trail

Locust Trail

N

Kilometer 0.5

Mile 0.5

Finding the trailhead: Follow U.S. Highway 30 east past Ligonier to the top of the summit. Turn right onto Laurel Summit Road and follow it about 2.2 miles to the ski hut and, across the street, a parking lot. *DeLorme: Pennsylvania Atlas and Gazetteer:* Page 73 C5. GPS coordinates N40 09.416 / W79 08.993

The Hike

Drive southwest along Laurel Summit Road from US 30 and you can't help but notice the signs for Laurel Mountain State Park.

Most think of it as a downhill ski area, and indeed it was the first major resort in western Pennsylvania at its birth in 1939. It opened to the public following World War II and turned the region into the "Ski Capital of Pennsylvania."

It's done well in some years since and closed for entire seasons at other times. What has never changed is that the park and adjacent Forbes State Forest offer some wonderful—and surprisingly easy—hiking. While the ski slopes drop about 700 feet, this trek is a flat, ridgetop walk.

There's a lot to see, though. In addition to mountain laurel and rock formations, white-tailed deer, black bears, coyotes, foxes, squirrels, turkeys, bobcats, and songbirds abound.

To begin, park your car in the "overflow" lot across from the Nordic ski patrol hut (a nice place to finish up in winter) and start hiking at the sign for Loop Trail. The trail winds through laurel and passes behind a private cabin until, at mile 0.2, coming to the foot of a rocky bluff. Turn left at this T.

You'll walk through open woods until, in the midst of some laurel at mile 0.6, coming to a small grade. Climb here and you'll come to a T at mile 0.7. To the right are the ski slopes and a maintenance area; instead, turn left. The woods here are thick with greenbrier, but it's kept cut back from the trail.

Mile 0.8 brings you to a junction with the Bill Alberts Trail. Follow the sign pointing TO LIPPOS LOOP, and in another 0.2 mile you'll come to a T; turn right.

The trail comes to yet another T at mile 1.4. This is the junction with Towhee Trail. Turn right, walk a few hundred feet, and turn left at another T to stay on Towhee. There are a few low-lying wet spots along this way, but they're nothing you can't bypass to keep your feet dry.

At mile 1.8 Towhee meets the Bill Alberts Trail. Turn right and go down a slight dip, with more rock formations on the right and lots of laurel, beautiful when it blooms in early to mid-June.

The Bill Alberts Trail meets Laurel Summit Road at mile 2.1. Turn left and return to your car, being sure to stop at the small pond on your left for a chance to see snakes, frogs, and other creatures.

Miles and Directions

0.0   Begin at the Loop Trail trailhead, which is marked by a wooden sign.

0.2   Look on the right to see a rocky bluff. Don't be surprised if you see a black bear, too, or at least their tracks in the snow; they live in fairly high densities all over this mountain-top.

0.8   At the junction with the Bill Alberts Trail, follow the signs directing you to Lippos Loop.

1.0   At the junction with Lippos Loop, turn right.

1.4   You'll turn right again at the junction with Towhee Trail. There are some low-lying wet spots in the trail here, but they can generally be avoided. A few hundred feet farther on, at a second junction with Towhee Trail, turn left.

1.8 Turn right when the trail meets up again with the Bill Alberts Trail. The trail here is adorned with mountain laurel and rhododendron, both of which bloom with large flowers in June.

2.1 Turn left when the trail meets Laurel Summit Road. Don't miss a chance to explore the pond on your left, though, as it's a good spot to see frogs, salamanders, snakes, and turtles.

2.3 Return to the parking area.

14 Quebec Run Wild Area

There are many beautiful hikes in western Pennsylvania, but it's hard to imagine any surpassing this loop through the Quebec Run Wild Area on Chestnut Ridge. Towering hemlocks, mountain laurel, two exquisite streams, and a variety of wildlife make this walk nothing short of amazing.

Start: The parking lot on Mill Run

Distance: 8.9-mile loop

Approximate hiking time: 4 to 5 hours

Difficulty: Moderate to difficult, with some hills and wet crossings

Trail surface: Dirt and rock paths and some forest roads

Seasons: Best hiked May to October

Other trail users: Hunters and bicyclists on the roads

Canine compatibility: Dogs permitted

Land status: State forest

Fees and permits: No fees or permits required

Schedule: Open year-round

Maps: Trail map available by contacting Forbes State Forest; USGS Bruceton and Bruceton Mills

Trail contacts: Forbes State Forest, Bureau of Forestry, Forestry District #4, P.O. Box 519, Laughlintown 15655; (724) 238-1200; www.dcnr.state.pa.us/forestry/stateforests/forbes.aspx

Special considerations: This is a beautiful hike at any time of year, but access to the parking area comes via a dirt road that can be very tough to negotiate in winter. It can be very treacherous in wet conditions, too.

Finding the trailhead: Take U.S. Highway 40 east to the top of the mountain and turn right onto Skyline Drive just past the Summit Inn. Go 6.6 miles, past the fire tower, and turn left onto the dirt Quebec Road. Go 2.5 miles, past the north parking lot, to a T and turn right. Park in the lot on the right just before crossing Mill Run. *DeLorme: Pennsylvania Atlas and Gazetteer:* Page 86 B1. GPS coordinates N39 45.821 / W79 39.819

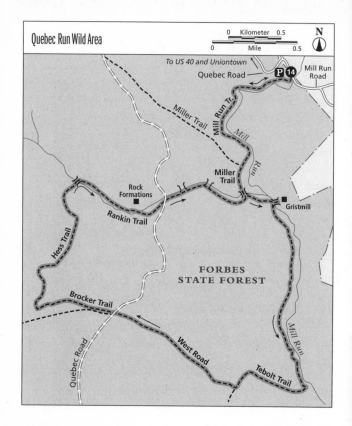

To US 40 and Uniontown
Quebec Road
Mill Run Road
Mill Run Tr.
Mill Run
Miller Trail
Miller Trail
Rock Formations
Rankin Trail
Gristmill
Hess Trail
FORBES STATE FOREST
Brocker Trail
Quebec Road
West Road
Mill Run
Tebolt Trail

The Hike

If there's a place where you can experience wilderness despite the once-heavy hand of man, Quebec Run Wild Area is it.

The nearly 7,500 acres that make up this portion of Forbes State Forest have been extensively logged at least twice, most recently seventy years ago. But you wouldn't know it to hike here. The wild area—which will never again see permanent development—is, quite simply, one of the most beautiful places in western Pennsylvania.

To begin, start at the Mill Run trailhead on Mill Run Road. The trail roughly parallels this stream for a while and can be wet in spring and fall with seeps and runoff.

At mile 1.1, when Mill Run Trail meets Miller Trail, turn left to stay on Mill Run. Mile 1.3 brings you to a junction with Rankin Trail; turn left to stay on Mill Run again, crossing the first of many Pennsylvania Conservation Corps bridges.

At mile 1.5 a bridge on the left crosses Mill Run and leads to the remains of a gristmill. Check that out, then backtrack to pick up this loop again, noticing the skunk cabbage, waterfalls, and hemlocks here.

You'll come to a sign directing you to go right to reach West Road and Tebolt Trail. Follow the sign, to mile 3.0, where Tebolt Trail goes left. Instead, continue straight to follow West Road. In another 0.2 mile, at a junction with Tebolt Road, turn right onto West Road again.

Bypass an unnamed road and you'll come to a junction with Quebec Road at mile 4.1. Cross the road, jog 30 yards uphill to the left, and reenter the woods at a sign for Brocker Trail/West Road. These trails split just 0.1 mile farther on; turn right onto Brocker.

You'll wind around a hillside that gets increasingly thick with rhododendron and laurel. At mile 4.8 you come to a T with the Hess Trail. Turn right to follow Hess, passing some yellow poplars.

You'll begin to follow Quebec Run at mile 5.8. Cross a bridge; then, at mile 6.4 you'll turn right onto Rankin Trail. Walking beneath towering hemlocks, you'll see Quebec Run on the right—shooting over long rock faces and between boulders half as big as a Volkswagen Beetle—and some rock formations on the left. It's a spectacular stretch of trail.

Next, cross straight over Quebec Road at mile 7.1. Cross two more bridges and, at mile 7.7, come to a junction with Miller Trail. Turn left, walk a few hundred yards, and then turn right onto Mill Run Trail to return to your vehicle.

Miles and Directions

0.0 Begin at the Mill Run trailhead. There's not a lot of space here, but crowds are rarely a problem either.

1.1 At the junction with Miller Trail, turn left to stay on Mill Run.

1.3 Turn left again at the junction with Rankin Trail to stay on Mill Run. This stream offers some good fishing under the hemlocks, if you're so inclined.

1.5 A spur here on the left leads to the ruins of a gristmill. What's left is mostly the stone foundation and some bits of wall, but it's still neat to see.

3.0 Go right onto West Road, which offers some easier walking.

4.1 Cross Quebec Road and, a few yards up the hill, turn onto Brocker Trail.

4.8 Turn right and head slightly downhill on Hess Trail.

6.4 Turn right at the junction with Rankin Trail and continue paralleling Quebec Run. This is one of the most scenic parts of this hike, so be sure to have a camera ready.

7.6 Turn left at a junction with Miller Trail and you're headed back to your car, retracing your steps over some ground covered previously.

8.9 Arrive back at the trailhead.

15 Ohiopyle State Park Ferncliff Peninsula

This hike winds through Ohiopyle State Park's Ferncliff Natural Area, a hundred-acre peninsula that's a National Natural Landmark. You'll likely see kayakers and rafters churning through rapids, get a bird's-eye view of the Yough from an old railroad bridge, and wander almost under the 30-foot Cucumber Falls.

Start: The Ferncliff Natural Area parking lot

Distance: 4.7-mile loop

Approximate hiking time: 2.5 to 3 hours

Difficulty: Easy to moderate, traversing generally flat terrain

Trail surface: Dirt and rock paths, with a short road section

Seasons: Best hiked April to October

Other trail users: Bicyclists in some sections

Canine compatibility: Dogs permitted, but they must be on a leash

Land status: State park

Fees and permits: No fees or permits required

Schedule: Open year-round

Maps: Map available by contacting Ohiopyle State Park; USGS Fort Necessity and Ohiopyle

Trail contacts: Ohiopyle State Park, P.O. Box 105, Ohiopyle 15470-0105; (724) 329-8591; www.dcnr.state.pa.us/stateparks/parks/ohiopyle.aspx

Special considerations: Archery hunting is allowed in Ferncliff Natural Area. There are a number of rapids in this section of the Yough, too, so use caution when around the river.

Finding the trailhead: The Ferncliff Natural Area parking area is reached by taking Route 381 south of Normalville to Ohiopyle. Turn right into the lot just before crossing over the Yough River. *DeLorme:*

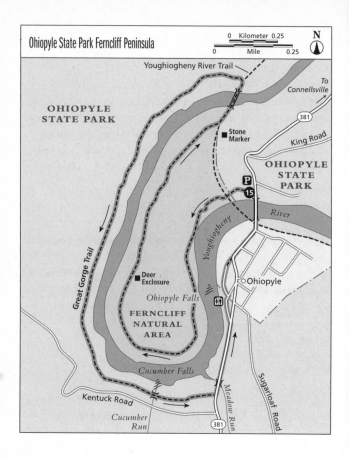

Ohiopyle State Park Ferncliff Peninsula

0 Kilometer 0.25

0 Mile 0.25

N

Youghiogheny River Trail

To Connellsville

381

King Road

OHIOPYLE STATE PARK

Stone Marker

P

15

OHIOPYLE STATE PARK

Youghiogheny River

Great Gorge Trail

Deer Exclosure

Ohiopyle Falls

FERNCLIFF NATURAL AREA

Ohiopyle

Cucumber Falls

Kentuck Road

Cucumber Run

Meadow Run

381

Sugarloaf Road

Pennsylvania Atlas and Gazetteer: Page 86 A3. GPS coordinates N39 52.311 / W79 29.646

The Hike

In the late 1880s, Ferncliff Natural Area was anything but natural. Entrepreneurs turned the peninsula into a regular

Coney Island, with a boardwalk, dance pavilion, ball fields, tennis courts, fountains, and hotel.

Today Ferncliff has largely returned to its natural state. It's a unique one, too. The Youghiogheny River, known as the "Yough" and pronounced "yock," flows north into Pennsylvania here, carrying seeds from Maryland and West Virginia. They get deposited on the peninsula and manage to survive—miles farther north than would typically be the case—because the river gorge is slightly warmer than the surrounding area.

To see that for yourself, park in the lot just north of the river on Route 381. Follow Ferncliff Trail into the natural area, following black blazes painted on rock. At mile 0.4 you'll come to a rocky point that offers a good look at the Ohiopyle Falls. A second vantage point exists at mile 0.5.

The trail Ys at mile 0.7; turn right and follow the trail markers. You'll pass a deer exclosure near mile 1.1 and, just beyond, come to a junction with Fernwood Trail. Turn left to stay on Ferncliff Trail.

The trail goes downhill next, leading to rock formations at the 1.5-mile mark and then through a grove of hemlocks.

Follow Ferncliff Trail until you can turn left onto the Yough River Trail. Follow it across a bridge, taking time to enjoy the view. Immediately after crossing the bridge, at mile 2.1, turn left onto the Great Gorge Trail, heavy with wildflowers in spring.

Ignore the yellow-blazed trail that goes to the left at mile 3.3 and continue to follow the Great Gorge Trail until reaching an iron bridge at mile 3.4. Turn left to cross the bridge, then make an immediate left to descend to the 30-foot Cucumber Falls.

Follow Cucumber Run downstream toward the river for about 0.1 mile, watching for Meadow Run Trail on the right. Turn here where the trail follows close by the river until, at mile 3.8, you come to a Y in the trail. Meadow Run Trail continues left; instead, go right and climb some steps to Route 381. Turn left and cross the bridge over Meadow Run and pass a snack bar and souvenir shop on your way through the main parking area. Along the way you can check out Ohiopyle Falls from this side of the river.

Once through the parking lot, cross the Yough one more time on the Route 381 bridge and return to your car.

Miles and Directions

0.0 Begin at the Ferncliff parking area and trailhead, which is also used by hikers and bikers who stick to the Yough River Trail.

0.5 Here, at some rocks, you get a good look at the Ohiopyle Falls from the side of the river opposite the traditional viewing area.

1.1 The trail passes a deer exclosure. White-tailed deer prefer to browse some tree species more than others—oaks are a favorite, for example, as compared to striped maple—and can literally change the composition of a forest if not controlled through hunting or fences, or both, as is the case here.

1.5 Rock formations form a natural cathedral.

1.7 A stone marker explains Ferncliff's natural and historical significance.

2.1 Turn left at the junction with Great Gorge Trail to get back into the woods.

3.4 Cucumber Falls rarely carries a lot of water to the Yough River, at least in summer, but it is a thing of beauty not to be missed nevertheless.

3.8 Turn right when Meadow Run Trail continues left and climb steps to Route 381.

4.7 Arrive back at the parking lot.

16 Flat Rock Trail

This hike is a relatively short one, but it's very scenic and pleasant to walk. And if you're feeling really adventurous, you can take a fast-paced dip into some startlingly refreshing—read cold—water.

Start: Adam Falls Picnic Area
Distance: 0.9-mile out-and-back
Approximate hiking time: 30 minutes
Difficulty: Easy, traversing a wide, almost perfectly flat trail
Trail surface: Dirt path
Seasons: Year-round
Other trail users: Picnickers and people with dogs
Canine compatibility: Dogs permitted, but they must be on a leash.
Land status: State park
Fees and permits: No fees or permits required
Schedule: Open year-round
Maps: Map available by contacting Linn Run State Park; USGS

Ligonier
Trail contacts: Linn Run State Park, P.O. Box 50, Rector 15677-0050; (724) 238-6623; www.dcnr.state.pa.us/stateparks/parks/linnrun.aspx
Special considerations: Glass containers are prohibited at the natural water slide at Flat Rock due to the wading that takes place there. Also, the park recommends exercising caution around the rocks, as several accidents occur each year. The rocks are very slippery—that's what makes them such a draw, after all—so when stepping on them, plan on getting wet. Those who don't are usually the ones who fall.

Finding the trailhead: Follow U.S. Highway 30 east for 2 miles past Ligonier. Turn south onto Route 381 and go 2 miles to the town of Rector. Turn left onto Linn Run Road and follow it into the park. The Adam Falls Picnic Area parking lot is the first one on the left. *DeLorme: Pennsylvania Atlas and Gazetteer:* Page 73 C5. GPS coordinates N40 10.163 / W79 14.015

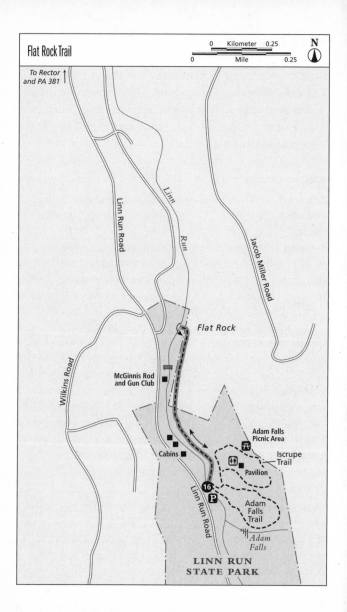

Flat Rock Trail

0 Kilometer 0.25

0 Mile 0.25

N

To Rector and PA 381 ↑

Linn Run Road

Linn Run

Jacob Miller Road

Flat Rock

McGinnis Rod and Gun Club

Wilkins Road

Cabins

Linn Run Road

Adam Falls Picnic Area

Iscrupe Trail

Pavilion

16

Adam Falls Trail

Adam Falls

LINN RUN STATE PARK

The Hike

It's not uncommon to be walking a trail and come across a tree with the initials of long-gone lovers carved into its bark. You'll even see a few while walking Flat Rock Trail.

It's more unusual to find initials carved into stone. But this trail has those, too.

As its name implies, Flat Rock Trail leads to a shelf of flat rock, 80 feet or more at its widest. Half of that is coated with a thin-to-the-point-of-being-invisible layer of algae and then the cold, spring-fed waters of Linn Run. The effect is a natural waterslide.

It's drawn picnickers for more than a century. Long before Linn Run was set aside as a state park in 1909, people were riding trains from nearby towns to slip and slide over the rocky streambed, dressed in wool suits that today look more like long johns than modern swimwear.

More than a few of those revelers carved dates and initials into the dry half of the streambed—a hump of sorts that parts the waters—and their handiwork is still there today, decades later.

To see that, and perhaps combine a hike with a picnic and a dip in the stream, start at the Adam Falls Picnic Area, a great place to have lunch or catch crayfish, minnows, and salamanders. A sign here identifies the trailhead.

Follow the trail as it parallels the stream, past beech, oak, and hemlock trees. Notice the rocky hillsides, so common in these mountains.

You'll see a few private cabins on your left, then at mile 0.3 climb a small hump. At the top, there's a trail backtracking to the right. Ignore it and continue on.

When you drop down the other side of the hump, just a

few steps farther along, you'll discover an old stone foundation, complete with a fireplace. That's the former McGinnis
Rod and Gun Club, abandoned since the 1940s.

Within a couple of dozen yards you'll find a log bench,
while mile 0.4 brings you to a bridge. Turn left, cross the
bridge, and you're at Linn Run's Flat Rock slide. Expect
to find lots of people here on warm, sunny weekends.
Children, teens, and adults in swimsuits and shorts will be
sliding over the rocks or sunning on them, while dogs frolic
on the edges.

Stop here, take in the view, perhaps wade or slide in the
stream, then turn and retrace your steps to the picnic area.

Miles and Directions

0.0 Begin at the Adam Falls Picnic Area, popular with families
because children can splash, look for crayfish, and generally
play in the always-cold waters of Linn Run.

0.3 Climb a small hump, the only rise on this otherwise flat
walk. Within a hundred yards or so, you'll see on your left
the remains of the old McGinnis Rod and Gun Club. Though
this area of the park is closed to hunting, it is bordered by
the Rolling Rock Club, an exclusive club that has played
host to former U.S. Vice President Dick Cheney and other
sporting dignitaries. Next, just past the club, you'll see a log
bench on the left side of the trail that offers a seat for those
looking to take a rest or just listen to the rush of Linn Run.

0.4 The bridge leading to Flat Rock is marked with a sign warn-
ing picnickers not to take glass bottles to the waterslide. This
is the turnaround point.

0.9 Return to the trailhead.

17 Wolf Rocks Trail

A lot of hikes promise to lead to scenic overlooks. Wolf Rocks Trail delivers. It takes you to a rocky outcrop nearly 100 feet wide and offers a magnificent view of the Linn Run Valley that's particularly stunning in the greens of summer and the reds, oranges, and yellows of fall.

Start: Laurel Summit Picnic Area

Distance: 4.5-mile loop

Approximate hiking time: 2 to 2.5 hours

Difficulty: Easy to moderate, due to flat terrain, but occasionally wet conditions and rocky trail surface

Trail surface: Dirt paths

Seasons: Year-round

Other trail users: Cross-country skiers and mountain bikers

Canine compatibility: Dogs permitted

Land status: State forest

Fees and permits: No fees or permits required

Schedule: Open year-round

Maps: Forest map available by contacting Forbes State Forest; park map available by contacting Laurel Summit State Park; USGS Ligonier

Trail contacts: Laurel Summit State Park, c/o Linn Run State Park, P.O. Box 50, Rector 15677-0050; (724) 238-6623; www.dcnr.state.pa.us/stateparks/parks/laurelsummit.aspx; Forbes State Forest, Bureau of Forestry, Forestry District #4, P.O. Box 519, Laughlintown 15655; (724) 238-1200; www.dcnr.state.pa.us/forestry/stateforests/forbes.aspx

Special considerations: The trailhead can be difficult to reach in winter. Linn Run Road does not get plowed (for the sake of snowmobilers), and while Laurel Summit Road does, this area can get a lot of snow.

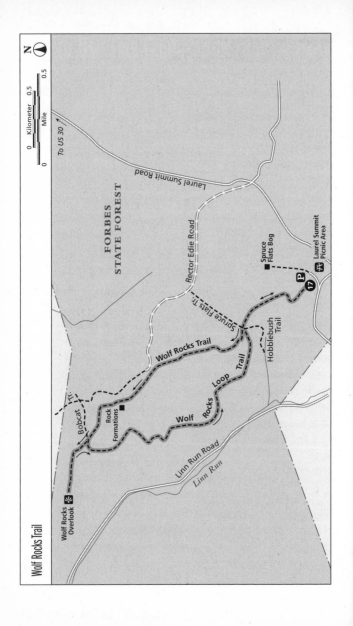

Wolf Rocks Trail

Finding the trailhead: Follow U.S. Highway 30 east past Ligonier to the top of the summit. Turn right onto Laurel Summit Road and follow it about 5 miles to a T. Turn right and pull into the Laurel Summit State Park. *DeLorme: Pennsylvania Atlas and Gazetteer:* Page 73 C5. GPS coordinates N40 07.105 / W79 10.595

The Hike

The launch point for Wolf Rocks Trail is deceiving. Situated in Laurel Summit State Park—six acres big, with one pavilion, a restroom, and a gravel parking lot—it's nondescript. The view at the end of this hike is nothing short of spectacular, however.

Look for the Wolf Rocks Trail sign at the edge of the parking lot. You'll notice sassafras here, along with mountain laurel. The trail is flat but rocky, with roots stretching across it like hardened veins.

In time you'll also encounter ferns, some of them growing waist high. They give sections of this hike an almost prehistoric feel.

At mile 0.5 you come to an intersection with Wolf Rocks Loop Trail and Spruce Flats Trail. You'll return via Wolf Rocks Loop later, so ignore these for now and continue straight on Wolf Rocks Trail.

Mile 0.7 brings you to the first of several welcome "bridges"—really elevated planks—that keep your feet dry by leading over wet spots in the trail.

Pass a plot of ferns in a sun-drenched opening in the woods at mile 0.8. Then, at mile 1.2, the trail splits. Turn left at a red marker to stay on Wolf Rocks Trail. You should be able to see woven wire fence, meant to keep deer out of an area foresters want to regenerate, on your right. If instead you find yourself on a logging road, you've missed the turn.

Look for an interesting rock formation on your left at mile 1.4.

The Wolf Rocks Loop Trail comes in on the left again at mile 1.9. Bypass it and continue straight on Wolf Rocks Trail, staying that course when Bobcat Trail comes in from the right a few hundred yards farther on.

At mile 2.2 you'll come to Wolf Rocks, an outcropping of Pottsville sandstone roughly 2,600 feet above sea level. Notice the evidence of frost cracks in the stone. There are signs of hikers having built fires here, too, but the area is remarkably free of litter and graffiti, so please keep it that way.

When you turn to go, backtrack to mile 2.5 until you can turn right onto Wolf Rocks Loop Trail, marked for much of its length by thick greenbrier.

You'll cross two seeps at mile 2.7. Continue on to mile 4.0, then turn right onto Wolf Rocks Trail (Hobblebush Trail, an expert mountain biking trail, is also here) and walk back to the starting point.

Miles and Directions

0.0 Begin at the Laurel Summit Picnic Area, which has one pavilion.

0.5 Continue straight at the junction with Wolf Rocks Loop Trail and Spruce Flats Trail.

0.7 Cross a small bridge—really an elevated platform—that serves to keep your feet dry at a chronic wet spot.

1.2 The trail bends left, away from a logging road. If you find yourself on the road, turn back.

1.4 Rock formations on both sides of the trail are a testament to the rocky countryside.

1.9 Continue straight at a junction with Wolf Rocks Loop. A few hundred yards farther on, you'll continue straight again at the junction with Bobcat Trail.

2.2 Arrive at the Wolf Rocks overlook, which is stunning at all times of year, but especially when the woods first green up in spring and again when they boast the reds, oranges, and golds of fall.

2.5 Turn right as you head out at the junction with Wolf Rocks Loop. The woods are thick with greenbrier here, so stick to the trail or risk some scratched shins.

4.0 Turn right at the junction with Wolf Rocks Trail to begin retracing your steps to your vehicle.

4.5 Return to the parking area, but don't leave until you take a side hike from here to see the Spruce Flats Bog, a unique habitat that supports a variety of interesting and rare, for this region, plants, such as cranberries and the carnivorous pitcher plant. Just be sure to minimize your impact by sticking to the boardwalk.

18 Laurel Hill State Park Loop

This loop hike in Laurel Hill State Park is a very pleasant one, winding through a maturing hardwood forest. Its best feature, though, is to be found near the end in the form of an engineering marvel that dates back seven decades or more.

Start: Laurel Hill State Park
Distance: 3.1-mile loop
Approximate hiking time: 1.5 to 2.0 hours
Difficulty: Easy to moderate, with a few gentle grades along wide, well-maintained paths
Trail surface: Dirt paths and gravel roads
Seasons: Year-round
Other trail users: Cross-country skiers, hunters, and snowmobilers
Canine compatibility: Dogs permitted, but they should be on a leash
Land status: State park

Fees and permits: No fees or permits required
Schedule: Open year-round
Maps: Map available by contacting Laurel Hill State Park; USGS Bakersville, Seven Springs, and Rockwood
Trail contacts: Laurel Hill State Park, 1454 Laurel Hill Park Road, Somerset 15501; (814) 445-7725; www.dcnr.state.pa.us/stateparks/parks/laurelhill.aspx
Special considerations: This hike wanders through woods that are open to hunting, so if you hike here in fall/winter, wear orange clothing.

Finding the trailhead: Laurel Hill State Park is located just off Route 31 near Bakersville. Take Route 3037 (Trent Road) from Route 31 to the park road. *DeLorme: Pennsylvania Atlas and Gazetteer:* Page 73 D5. GPS coordinates N40 00.362 / W79 14.715

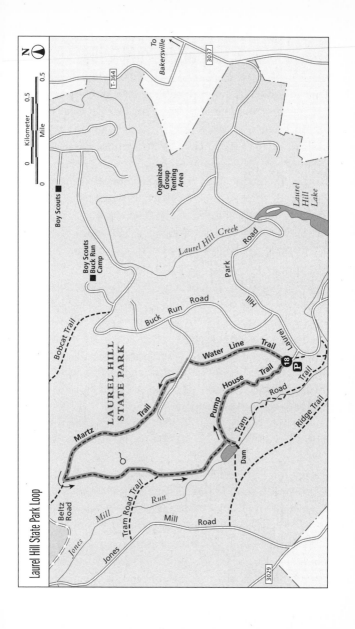

The Hike

Usually, the most scenic places are those untouched by the hand of man. This is not one of those places.

The most spectacular highlight of this loop hike is a dam on Jones Mill Run that was built by the young men of the Civilian Conservation Corps during the Great Depression.

Between 1933 and 1945, CCC crews built roads, bridges, and buildings in state parks all across Pennsylvania. They spent a lot of time in Laurel Hill State Park. It was then one of five sites in the state designated as recreational demonstration areas by the National Park Service, and today still contains the largest collection of CCC architecture to be found in state parks. The dam on Jones Mill Run was one of the park's signature projects, and it remains a place of magical beauty today, as you'll see.

To begin, park in the lot for the Pump House Trail trailhead. Go around the gate and bear right, following the signs for Water Line Trail. This is a snowmobile route—all the legs of this loop are—so it's wide and well-maintained. It passes through a maturing forest that's a mottled gray and green thanks to the countless mossy granite boulders.

The trail climbs gradually if steadily until coming to a T with a forest road at mile 0.6. Turn left, following the sign for Martz Trail/Beltz Trail.

Another sign at mile 1.0 directs you to continue straight ahead—past a giant blue water tower—on Martz Trail. The forest understory is largely mountain laurel initially, changing over to greenbrier as you go along.

At mile 1.5, turn left onto Pump House Trail at a sign. This trail is narrower and a bit rocky for a while; water naturally courses down the trail in spring. You'll notice a small spring on your left at mile 1.9 and Jones Mill Run in the valley on your right.

The trail Ys at mile 2.5. Pump House Trail goes left, and that's the way you'll go to complete this hike. First, though, turn right and walk a few hundred feet to the dam on Jones Mill Run. It's made of huge blocks of rough-cut stone, stacked stair-step style. The white water of Jones Mill Run stands out in stark contrast to the dark chocolate stone as it Slinkies its way over it and onward.

When you're ready to go, backtrack to Pump House Trail and turn right. You'll bypass a trail on the right at mile 3.0 leading to the park's campground and cottages and arrive back at the trailhead at mile 3.1.

Miles and Directions

0.0 Begin at the Pump House Trail trailhead, which is well marked with a sign. Note, though, that you won't start out on Pump House Trail. Instead, you'll make an immediate right onto Water Line Trail and return via Pump House Trail later.

0.6 After a long and steady uphill climb, the trail meets with a gravel road. Turn left, away from a gate, to follow the road.

1.0 Arrive at a sign for Martz Trail and a large blue water tower that stands on the right, just beyond the sign.

1.5 Turn left at the junction with Pump House Trail. The trail goes downhill on a course that's often wet with runoff and always rocky.

1.9 Look on the left for a natural spring.

2.5 The trail Ys here. You'll ultimately go left to return to your vehicle, but first turn right to see the dam on Jones Mill Run. There is a bench here and plenty of natural rock seats, so this is a wonderful place to enjoy a picnic lunch, read a book, fish, or just relax.

3.1 Return to the trailhead parking lot. If you want to cool down with a swim after hiking or have a picnic, turn right as you exit the lot to get to Laurel Hill Lake, which features a beach surrounded by pavilions, picnic tables, and plenty of open space to toss a Frisbee or football.

Clubs and Trail Groups

Allegheny Group of the Sierra Club
The closest Sierra Club chapter to Pittsburgh. Members hail from the city and outlying areas and do a lot of hiking in the Laurel Highlands and the areas north of the city. For information contact P.O. Box 8241, Pittsburgh, PA 15217; alleghenysc.org; www.alleghenysc.org.

Allegheny Outdoor Club
This is a group of hikers, bikers, and skiers/snowshoers in northwestern Pennsylvania. Outings are scheduled weekly. For information contact John and Debra Young, 1588 Town Line Road, Russell 16345; (814) 757-8158; John .Young@madbbs.com; www.alleghenyoutdoorclub.org.

Audubon Society of Western Pennsylvania
This group not only operates Beechwood Farms Nature Reserve and Todd Nature Reserve but also leads hikes there and provides a variety of nature programming. For information contact ASWP, 614 Dorseyville Road, Pittsburgh, PA 15238; (412) 963-6100; www.aswp.org.

Butler Outdoor Club
This group schedules activities ranging from hiking to canoeing to nature skills. Some are run by the club; at other times, club members travel together to take part in activities run by state parks, for example. For information contact Butler Outdoor Club, P.O. Box 243, Butler, PA 16003-0243; president@butleroutdoorclub.org; www.butlerout doorclub.com.

Friends of Raccoon Creek State Park

This group maintains trails in Raccoon Creek State Park and coordinates outings there. It is also affiliated with nearby Hillman State Park. For information e-mail email@Friendsof Raccoon.com or visit www.friendsofraccoon.com.

Keystone Ramblers

A hiking organization that leads hikes of four types: relaxed hikes of less than 10 miles over moderate ground; hard-core hikes of more than 8 miles requiring a vigorous pace; path-of-progress hikes that explore Pennsylvania's industrial past; and heritage hikes that explore sites of natural or historical significance. For information e-mail keystone-ramblers@ worldnet.att.net or visit http://keystone-ramblers.home.att .net.

Keystone Trails Association

This is the state's largest hiking organization. It organizes outings and is a leading advocate for hiking concerns. For information contact 101 North Front Street, Harrisburg 17101; (717) 238-7017; ktahike@verizon.net; www.kta-hike.org.

North Country Trail Association

This group, which has several chapters in Pennsylvania, promotes and maintains the section of the North Country Trail that runs across the Keystone State. For general information and details on the various chapters in Pennsylvania, visit www.northcountrytrail.org/explore/ex_pa/ pa.htm. For details on the Butler County Chapter (which deals with the trail in Moraine and McConnells Mill State Parks), write Butler Chapter, NCTA, Box 2968, Butler, PA

16001; call Ron Rice at (724) 538-8475; or e-mail nctpa@ zbzoom.net. For details on the Wampum Chapter (which deals with the trail where it runs across Game Lands 285 and elsewhere), e-mail Gail Blakeley at gail2@zoominternet.net or Bill Majernik at WIJOMA@aol.com.

Rachel Carson Trails Conservancy

This is the organization that promotes and maintains the Rachel Carson Trail and Baker Trail in southwestern Pennsylvania. For information contact Rachel Carson Trails Conservancy Inc., P.O. Box 35, Warrendale, PA 15086-0035; (412) 366-3339; info@rachelcarsontrails.org; www .rachelcarsontrails.org.

Venture Outdoors

A nonprofit organization based in Pittsburgh, Venture Outdoors organizes a whole host of outdoor programs, from guided hikes to kayak trips to fly-fishing classes. There is a fee for most programs, but you get a discount if you become a member. For information contact Venture Outdoors, 304 Forbes Avenue, Second Floor, Pittsburgh 15222; (412) 255-0564; www.ventureoutdoors.org.

Western Pennsylvania Conservancy

The conservancy operates Bear Run Nature Reserve and its network of trails. It also purchases property that it then sells to state agencies at below-market prices. A number of state park, forest, and game lands tracts have come into existence this way. For information contact Western Pennsylvania Conservancy, 800 Waterfront Drive, Pittsburgh 15222; (412) 288-2777; www.paconserve.org.

Westmoreland Bird and Nature Club
Though primarily a birding organization, this group leads hikes, runs nature programs, and does other activities that are of interest to people who love the outdoors. For information contact Rose Tillmann, Box 188, New Derry, PA 15671; www.westol.com/~towhee/wcbc.htm.

Yough River Trail Corp.
This is the group that takes care of the 43-mile northern section of the Yough River rail trail that includes the section between West Newton and Smithton. For information contact Regional Trail Corporation, 111 Collinsburg Road, West Newton 15089; (724) 872-5586; www.youghriver trail.com.

About the Author

Bob Frye is the outdoors editor for Pittsburgh's *Tribune-Review* newspaper. He is the author of *Best Hikes Near Pittsburgh* (FalconGuides) and *Deer Wars: Science, Tradition, and the Battle over Managing Whitetails in Pennsylvania,* and he has written numerous outdoor articles for national and regional magazines. Born and raised in western Pennsylvania, he has hiked, fished, camped, and photographed wildlife and nature throughout much of the region's forests and fields, including hiking and backpacking trips with his sons, Derek and Tyler, and wife, Mandy. He lives in North Huntingdon.